CRUCIFIXION PART 2,
ONLY THIS TIME
WE'RE COMING FOR YOU!

IT JUST HAD TO BE HEARD

Presents

CRUCIFIXION PART 2, ONLY THIS TIME WE'RE COMING FOR YOU!

By

BISHOP KATRINA T. SMITH

Print information available on the last page.

Rev. date: 08/26/2022

To order additional copies of this book, contact:
Xlibris
844-714-8691
www.Xlibris.com
Orders@Xlibris.com
822627

Table of Contents

GOD GAVE ME A GIFT THAT I NOW SHARE WITH YOU

WELCOME TO THE NEW YOU!
Pass this book of Good News to all you know
and watch your breakthrough!
GOD Chose You as His Own
Read this book straight through and WELCOME HOME!
Words of thanks to all who helped me
As for I, greater blessings you too shall see
And to My Earth
My gracious Mother who brought me birth
I share to the world just how much I love you
I thank God Mommy for you are my breakthrough!
And to You, My Dear Reader, and Listener
I promise, you discover a New You in each chapter
For sure,
You Have Been Called Now for; WE ARE AT WAR!

Chapter 1

GOD'S FRONTLINE SOLDIERS!

"Thou therefore endure hardness, as a good soldier of Jesus Christ. No man that warreth entangleth himself with the affairs of this life; that he may please him who hath chosen him to be a soldier." (2 Timothy 2:3-4 KJV)

"I have given them thy word; and the world hath hated them, because they are not of the world, even as I am not of the world. "I pray not that thou shouldest take them out of the world, but that thou shouldest keep them from the evil." (John 17:14-15 KJV)

"Put on the whole armor of God, that you may be able to stand against the wiles of the devil. For we do not wrestle against flesh and blood, but against principalities, against powers, against the rulers of darkness in this age, against spiritual hosts of wickedness in the heavenly places." (Ephesians 6:11-13 KJV)

Crucifixion

PART

"2"

ONLY THIS TIME

SATAN

WE'RE COMING FOR YOU!

GOD'S FRONTLINE SOLDIERS

I told you

That I would return

It's time to infiltrate Hell's camp

Sending those demons back to the origin in

which their souls were destined to burn!

WOMEN GUARD THE GATE!

You hold the key to deliverance for it is in

your seed that determines Satan's fate

Let it be said,

That what you birth has the potential to

bruise Satan's heel and head!

GOD'S LEADING LADIES GOD'S LEADING MEN

TO ALL

A call

Has been made in your name!

GOD is ready to claim victory on Earth

This is why you were granted the blessing of birth

Your Choice

Death or Life

Sin or Win

Our counterattack on Hell has begun

Yet,

This is a battle that you can't fight yourself or no one else

YOU MUST LET GOD IN!

NOW

KEEP IT REAL!

Satan tried his mightiest to steal to kill your life to blind your sight

To rape your dream

His most deadly weapon is to divide our army turning

Man against man

Team against team

Yet,

We Must Stand and Band as One

The peak of this war has already begun

I see a frown, let me break this down!

FIRST!

TO STOP THIS CURSE

PUT YOURSELF ASIDE!

For, death doesn't care about what material things you have

Your house, your mate, or your luxury ride!

JUST HEED FOR GOODNESS' SAKE!

While I analyze man's future generation

The fate of this nation if we continue at this rate!

PLAGUES

Your Women

Your seed breeders are abundantly dying from Aids!

Which by the way if I may say is a manmade disease!
You see!
Satan knows like the Jews in the Holocaust
that the women hold the keys!
To man's extinction of their race!
Don't you dare block out this knowledge
for the truth you must embrace!

LET'S TALK ABOUT YOUR NEXT IN KIN!
Satan is completely destroying your men!
Having them believe
That selling drugs or committing a crime is
their only path in order to succeed
A quick shine
Poisoning their own community
Growing off the misery of others whose souls were left behind
To fail!
Didn't you know that you were building up Satan's army in Hell!

MOST CRUCIAL!
Your life support
Your main artery bleeds
For Satan has used your media your entertainers
to help corrupt your own Seeds!

THEY LUST FOR WORLDLY THINGS!
Cars, clothes, sex, drugs, guns, jewelry, and diamond rings
Wiser yet Weaker
Yet, who's to blame?
They're dying to live in the spotlight and claim their fame!

Yet, there are many of the rich who sold
their souls now living in shame!
LOST!
DON'T YOU KNOW BECAUSE OF YOUR SELFISH
ACT ALL MANKIND WILL PAY THE COST!

It's time to stop and drop those negative words!
Let the truth GOD'S teachings be heard throughout this world!
Let's stop worrying about dollars and protect the
innocence of our young boys and girls!
I AM NOT AFRAID TO DIE!
Yet, I am afraid to live every day as Satan's puppet enduring a lie!

THIS WAR!
Has been since the Garden of Adam and Eve
It may look that way, but Satan is not in the lead!

NOW HEED!
It Starts at Home You Must Atone!
It Starts with You
Get Baptized in Christ's Blood Allow Him to Work Through You!

THE LORD SPEAKS!
MY CHILD I GRANTED YOU FREEDOM OF CHOICE
NOW THE DECISION IS YOURS TO
FOLLOW YOUR INNER VOICE!

My Brothers and Sisters
IN THE NAME OF JESUS
If you want to enroll in GOD'S Army today

REPEAT THIS AND SAY

THIS CRUCIFIXION IS PART 2 ONLY THIS TIME SATAN
THIS SOLDIER IS COMING AFTER YOU!

AMEN, SO LET IT BE DONE!
WELCOME
YOU ARE THE CHOSEN ONE!

Sing a New Song
Sing about the Glory of God's Strong Arm

Tell My Children That
It Won't Be Long

I'm coming back to claim those that honored
and feared My Sovereign Name
Scripture proclaims, *"That we are sure of this because*
Christ rose from the dead and he will never die again.
Death no longer has any power over him.
He died once to defeat sin and now he lives for the Glory of God."
Tell My Children that I'm Coming Back to
Give What the Devil Tried to Rob!
What he tried to steal
Scripture says, *"I snatched back from the jaws of death so*
know that all your infirmities shall be healed by your faith."
Tell My Children
That I hold the keys of death and the grave so constantly
raise up My Name with your highest thanks!
I AM That I AM what pieces all together
Scripture says, *"That I will swallow up death forever!"*
I will remove all your sorrows, there will
be no more crying or pain
I AM the First and the Last
Those that love death know not My Name
Tell My Children That It Won't Be Long
That you will find shelter throughout each storm
That I will cover you with My Strong Arm!

Tell My Children to trust in Me at all times
That what they seek they shall surely find
It's Time to Raise from My Throne It's
Time to Sing a New Song

TELL MY CHILDREN THAT
IT WON'T BE LONG!

Who Is God?

He is the Creator of all things who dwells
in both Heaven and Earth

He is the reason why you were granted birth

He is all knowing yet He gives you the freedom of choice

He is your mentor guiding you through your inner voice

He is the air that allows you to breathe

He is the rock of time which you stand on in order to succeed

He is your guiding light always drawing you towards right

He is the arm of shelter

Your Shining Knight that protects and
comforts you through the night

He is the one that dries your tears a
Divine Spirit that all must fear

He is the food that nourishes the fertilizer
that flourishes forever

He is the problem solver

That piece by piece builds your puzzle together

He is never to be taken for granted once your seeds are planted

He is you and you are He

It's in your Soul where He longs to be

Yet,

You must let Him in

Only then will the new you in Christ begin

Who Is God You Say?

Surrender to Him and all your answers
will be patiently delivered

Receiving victory day by day

Let Him Through

He's In

You!

True

Nothing to hide
I'm laying my burdens down side by side
and Worship You Lord
RABBONI,
My Master of All High
My Burden Taker Hear My Silent Cry
Thank you, Father, for the air I breathe
Thank you, Father, for creating me to succeed
I have the force to move mountains instilled within me
I have the strength and knowledge to make my dreams a reality
Yet,
I must believe in myself
Dedicating my life to You and no one else!
You are the fertilizer that allows me to grow
The wisdom of eternity that I seek to know
THANK YOU, FATHER,
Thank You, Father, for Choosing Me
Thank You, Father, for No Matter How Terrible
I Was Goodness You Could Still See
Now, I fall down on my knees shouting in rejoice!
For, I finally made the right choice
Lord, I Pray Hear My Voice!
If I must die with what I have now one thing is true
FATHER
With All That I Am I Love You
I Need You, I Worship You, and I Would Die for You
For,
You Are and Forever Will Be
TRUE!

12

This Message Has Been Sent
Voices Of Repent!

First, We Claim the Lord as Our Savior for His Life He Gave
Now, We Must Repent in Order to Be Saved
FATHER,
We Throw to You Our Sins For This Is
Where The Promise Begins

I confess that I have cheated on my mate
Father, I ask for forgiveness of this mistake
I confess that I have corrupted my body with smoke
Inhaling that drug until I choke
I confess that I have infested my body with sex
Sharing with the next and the next
I confess that I have said unkind words
Filled with hatred after hearing the negativity that I heard
I confess that I have taken for granted life
Finding more pleasure in wrong than right
I confess that I have deceived making others not believe
I confess that I have stolen taking from
others that which wasn't mine
Father, I confess my crime!
I confess that I have sold drugs
Taking life from others hanging out in
the streets with the local thugs
I confess that I have lived in selfishness
Only praising those that granted my every wish
I confess that I have been stingy with my money

With the blessings that You gave to me

I didn't care about the low lives on the streets that I see

FATHER,

The list goes on and on for every day we sin

Yet,

It's our destiny to win!

So,

We Raise Up Our Voices of Repent

Until our Souls are sent

Until we meet face to face

Until Your forgiveness we embrace

To You That Reads and Listens This Message Has Been Sent!

For,

Now

It's Your Turn To

REPENT!

A
Starving Soul!

I had to fall down on my knees tonight
Asking God
For the strength and courage to survive life
To bless me with insight
To ease this internal battle between wrong and right
You see,
I'm recognizing that I'm not living as God would want me
Tears fell,
Spiritually, physically, emotionally, financially,
and mentally I'm not doing well
I'm overwhelmed,
Surrounded by negative energy my soul is not properly fed
Feeling as if there's no peace to clear my head
I want to run, running to that which relieves my pain
So, I can laugh and have fun
Yet, at the day's end
A more self-disappointing attitude has just begun
Terrorists are after me,
Eating away at my flesh targeting my soul hindering me
From being all I can be
Honestly,
Sometimes I feel like my worst enemy
My most harmful terrorist is I
You see,
It's time to accept the truth rather than live a lie
Every decision

It was my choice!

Denying the wisdom of my inner voice

One thing is a fact

I want to get back on track!

I yearn to live right

Yet,

As the thought enters my mind temptation blinds my sight

This is a constant fight that I must undergo

However, there's something that I know

That I must feed my soul, have faith, and wait on the Lord

For,

The Devil

Is Already Defeated

Heed It!

I'm Still Here!

You may tear me down with your vicious hand
Yet, like the rocks that survived the test of time I will stand!
Let me share,
I'm Still Here!
You may damage my name deter my fame
Yet, through the Blood of Christ victory I will claim
I overcame
My fear
I'm Still Here!
You may deceive me to believe
That my destiny in life I shall not succeed
That I can't provide my own needs
Yet, I will not be a follower I will lead
Because I care
I'm Still Here!
For a fact,
You may stab me in my back
Throw my obedience to God off track
Make me forget
How a virtuous woman and man are supposed to act!
Yet,
Like a puzzle my Lord keeps my pieces intact!
Death was near
Yet, through faith
I'M STILL HERE!

Walk Into Your Worth!

I CAN HEAR MY LORD SAY,
I COME TO YOU THE LOWLY I COME TO YOU THE SINNER
FOR, I HEARD YOUR CRY!

This is for you my battered woman
This is for you my lost son
This is for you my hungry child searching for
someone to heal your broken heart
Now, where shall I start?

I need you to understand
Put not all your faith in any man
For man's love changes as the seasons flow
If you choose to grow
You must first let go of all that which hinders your growth
My child I will move in your worth!
I am My Word and My Word is Me
How can you speak to your storm in My Name without
being able to quote my Word on your reality?
Other words, you must study Me to fulfill your destiny!

I know your issues that you currently embrace
I see the endless pain that you're forced to face
But this my child was meant to make you strong
It was meant to show you that I can prevail over any storm!
Don't you see
That with every trial and tribulation you grew closer to Me!
The Almighty

I have shown you that I am your only true provider
That can take you higher
That I Am your only true healer
That even made many say no to their drug dealers
That I Am your only true friend
That even when others left, I carried you until the end
That I Am your only true redeemer
That erased your doubts and made you a true believer
That I Am your only true that I Am!

You were not meant to be like others so stop comparing
You were not blessed financially just for
your pleasures so start sharing
You were not given life to turn your back on Jesus Christ
You are You!
Surrender all and I will direct you on what to do
For then you will be My vessel where My Holy Spirit shall dwell
Never stop trying for if you do you will be giving glory to hell
Where your soul shall forever dwell
No!
It's not too late actually you're right on time
Seek Me first and the truth you shall find

HEAVEN HERE ON EARTH!
WALK INTO YOUR WORTH!

God Is Moving It All In Your Favor!

You will have victory
Over your enemies even the enemy that lives
in me and your so-called neighbors
Smiling in your face while all along plotting to destroy you
But, like Jesus Judas was used for the favor of His breakthrough!
Thank God for the no's and the tears
And the late-night thoughts that kept you in fear
Thank God for the hurt, for returning my good with dirt, for
their vicious lies, for those silent cries, and negative comments
Pay close attention for this was meant
What you don't kill will eventually kill you
Stand up and lead my people through
God chose YOU!
That is why you are hated on because you are the breakthrough!
God said,
I watched you
I saw what others are unable to see
This is why it's My honor to crown you
from the Lord of Heaven's Armies
Today, is not just an ordinary day!
Today, the universal from above, below, and beyond shall see
The wrath of God our Almighty
For, the enemy came up against the wrong person a Child of God
And for the sake of His Name, no good thing shall be robbed
You will have victory
Over all your enemies even the enemy that lives
in me and your so-called neighbors!

God Is Moving It All In Your Favor!

I Got Evidence!

Pay close attention for this was meant

Was it not God who parted the Red Sea?

So, know that when your enemy is chasing after you

God already made an escape route to victory

Hear me

Was it not Jesus who gave His life?

So, know that God only sees you in your true light

God's strength is made perfect in weakness so know that

He has already arranged your wrongs right

I do tell

Was it not God who called David from the sheep pens

making him the shepherd of God's own people, Israel?

So, do know that greatness is born in darkness

That each day you live

Live to give and focus on the good and not the useless

For, was it not God who carried you through?

The sickness, broken heart, lack, and suicidal thoughts too

Had it not been for God where would I be

I'm telling the world that God kept me!

I should have been dead

But God's strong right arm led

Me to safety

I got evidence every day of how God loves me!

Now, the time is yours to make

God your only Savior for your own soul's sake

Don't fake

Jesus died for all our sins so know that no man is

perfect that is never a reason to not let God in

Live to win

And I promise that you too will say

This is not a coincidence!

This is just another blessing from God so that I can say

I Got Evidence!

Turning Lemons into Lemonade

Making positivity out of shade

Or hate

Take heed to these words for they will change your fate

When life gives you lemons or sour

Know that this is your hour

To make lemonade by adding water or love,

sugar or kindness, and if desired ice

Focus on the good in life

While laboring to improve

Dancing to your own new groove

Be You!

Beautiful, talented, loving, intelligent, strong,

highly-flavored, and kindhearted too

Love You!

You have what it takes to succeed

Just believe

In that which dwell in You

Break your breakthrough

And trust that whatever is needed has been already made!

So, when life throws you lemons just smile and make

LEMONADE!

God Lifted Me Up!

For His Own Name Sake God redirected my
fate and loosed all which was stuck
As if to say, "Enough is Enough!"
Praise our Holy Trinity our Father, God, Spirit
for the Word sent out as I speak!
Scripture says, "and I will be a Father to you, and you
shall be sons and daughters to Me says the Lord Almighty
My Strength is made perfect where you are weak!"
For you are all sons of God through faith in Christ Jesus
A Name Above all names sent to lead us
For if God be for us who or what can be against us
Only in our Savior Christ Jesus we place our trust
I speak the Word over all that which is weak the enemy
even the enemy in me must return what was robbed!
Scripture says, "Therefore you are no longer a slave,
but a son, and if a son, then an heir through God!"
Give me what is rightfully mine to have right now on this Earth!
I draw to me things and people that will help me birth
That which leads all into their true worth
God shall supply all our needs
But Jesus said, "Let the children alone, and do not
hinder them from coming to Me for the Kingdom
of Heaven belongs to such as these"
Scripture says, "All your sons will be taught of the Lord
and the well-being of your sons will be great."
So, rest assured that the Word of God goes out and never
returns voids and you are right on time and not late

Just spend more time progressing instead of
resting and worrying about the hate
Not because of me
I'm telling the world that God changed my reality
For His Name's sake
Yes, the Lord redirected my fate
And pulled me out of all which was stuck!
I'm telling the world that I should have been dead but

God Lifted Me Up!

BECAUSE HE KNEW THAT I HAD ENOUGH!

My final share,
God doesn't give you more than you can bear

In Jesus Christ's Matchless Name Amen
Glory be unto God begin!
Live to deny sin!
LET GOD IN TO WIN!
AMEN!

Hallelujah Anyhow

Praise The Lord Even When You're Down!

My Lord of All High
I'm going to praise you until my tears dry
Until I cease my last breath
Lord your praise will ring until my death
Father,
I have been punished severely in this pit
Talked about broken down and kicked
Left for dead
No avenues to move ahead
Yet,
Hallelujah Anyhow
Lord, I'm going to continue to praise you even when I'm down
I have sinned in your sight
I have deliberately chosen wrong and not right
Yet, I was not granted life to live in strife
So, I confess
Praying that you care no less
Towards me
It's my ultimate goal to see
Your face
Father, until our Souls embrace
My money is drained out
My mind has me living in doubt
Bills are due
Who would have known?
That I would be on welfare

I guess we all have our time to share without

Hallelujah Anyhow

Lord, I shout!

I may look a mess

I may have to continue to wear this old dress

Yet, Lord I confess

Hallelujah Anyhow

For my time is coming to obtain my best

To you that listen or read

If you want to succeed

Throughout this storm of life

Shout this to everyone in sight

Hallelujah Anyhow

Praise the Lord Even When You're Down!

I need you to heed what the Word said

That

Faith Without Works is Dead!

Now this may not make you happy

You may not jump up out of your seats

But I tell you,

That praising the Lord without purposeful

movement topped with a strong belief

Can still have you dwelling in defeat

Why?

Because your everyday reality and destiny must meet!

So, what do you do?

You have to plan and labor for your own breakthrough

God said, "Seek and you shall find knock and I shall come"

But it is the first step of your own needed for

you to know that the process has begun

Tell me,

Why is it that even women in labor must

push with a strong degree of pain

For new life to be claimed?

In other words, you have to build while claiming in Jesus' Name

Nothing is free

So, if you want change then you must be willing

to fight to fulfill your true prophecy

Even the Lord said, "That the harvest is

plenty, but the laborers are few"

You want to know why because many

are not willing to do the work

Which they have to do
To make their dreams come true!
Don't get happy saying how much we love you Lord
Expecting our God to give you more
Just because I claim
I tell you it's a shame
That many will not see thou Kingdom Come
Heaven on Earth
Because they had 55 million excuses why
they can't walk into their worth
I tell you, don't return to dirt
Without laboring without sacrificing
Without being patient
For the Word surely said
That Your Faith Without Works Is Dead!
Give
Live for what it takes
Now this should make you happy
My Child you are not a mistake!
God said make one move and I shall change your fate
I need you to heed what this word just now said

That Faith Without Works is Dead!

You're In His Name

I have to be honest
Allowing the truth to spread
Lord, I haven't lived with You as my complete head
Father, I led
A life with selfish gratification
I made wrong choices because of my impatience
I was running for fame
Working endless hours to obtain materialistic things
Father!
As the tears fall
I gave many, yet I never gave You my all!
I was afraid to change; Lord I didn't believe I could grow strong
I'll admit that I lost something, I lost faith in the midst of my storm
Every day that I live
I become more aware of the pattern
Of the sinful cycle dwelling over my life
Lord!
Only You can turn my wrongs right!
I confess,
That I grew content with less
That I was attacked by the enemy when I tried my best
Nevertheless, You still loved me
You still forgave me
You remained when others left
Lord!
I confess that I need your Holy Spirit to come upon me
Only then will I witness the fulfillment of my true destiny!
With my head bowed and heart opened to claim

I now accept that my freedom comes only

IN YOUR NAME!

Raise me

Save me

Dwell in me

Teach me to let go

Father allow me to grow

On this day, Lord I pray

Erase my shame

IN JESUS NAME

Amen

In My Belly

Rages an internal battle between wrong and right
You see,
In order to live Christ like I have to change my life
I have to release loved ones and friends that don't believe
I have to relinquish all the things that I have come to need
I can't allow my body, my holy temple to be touched
I have to let go of man and trust
Only in the Lord
In my belly I feel an urge to be more
It shakes me it convicts me
It wants to come out yet, first I must let go of the old me
I know that I am not alone
No! There are many right now feeling the same as I do
Who wants to let go and follow the Holy True?
Yet, hell doesn't want to let go
Hell wants to keep you so that you die lost
Well, I tell you my people we can't afford that cost!
Just drop it!
Tell that person goodbye
Throw away that liquor and deadly high
Don't look back grow stronger for the Lord
And He will raise you up
Release that stuck mentality
Stop dreaming and walk into your true reality
MY LORD SAID
That everything that you need I fed into your belly
Your strength dwells there

My Holy Spirit lives there

Hear!

Receive what is said today in this message I give

To live is to live only for Me

Birth what I placed in your belly

My Chosen Child

Come out of the wild

Fast, pray, ask

And it shall surely come

Let Me dwell in your belly

My Faithful One

Amen

You have to die to yourself daily in order to win

My eternal light
Release it lay it down on Me tonight!

A Woman's Prayer

I've been
Looking for the security of men
To answer my quest in life
I have laid down my holiest between their sheets at night
Yet, it still didn't bring me joy and fulfillment
It still didn't right my wrongs

I've been praying for deliverance, yet still living the same
I've been seeking for someone to agree
with me to help ease my shame
I've been lazy
Procrastinating
Complaining that others are hating
But it's me!
I came to realize that I am my own worst enemy!
So, what shall I do?
I can get rid of people, yet how do I get rid of you
How do I get rid of myself?
How do I allow myself to grow to be someone else?

THE LORD SPEAKS
I hung from a cross
So that your soul would not be lost
I performed numerous miracles so that you would believe
I gave you my Word to feed all your needs

Yet, you of little faith
Bow down and give Me Thanks!
Why?
Why is it that the answer to all your questions you already know?
Yet you have a fear of letting go
I told you that you would not be alone
That I would journey with you all the way
until you receive my eternal home
Yet, watch you walk away
You're not fully ready to heed what I say
Yet, you surely will one day
You will fall to your knees
You will shout Lord please!
Because you haven't experienced enough pain
To let go and claim my HOLY NAME
Yet, it will come
It is already written my Chosen One
Live one day at a time
The truth my merciful grace you shall find
Rebuke the devil and he shall flee
Surrender all and follow Me!
All that you dream you shall See!
Amen
So let it be done
You will lead
My Chosen One

Look Beyond The Green

Your Inner Voice Screams
To Be Set Free
Beyond the green lies your destiny!

I heard you express your passion your once known dream
I heard that you quit because it wasn't as easy as it seems
You created in your mind why continuing
would be a waste of time
Plus, you didn't have the money to build it the way you saw fit
Once again, another reason to quit
It's funny how we can make ourselves available
for others instead of doing what is necessary
I hope you hear me!
It's funny how on Sunday you find work to do
Knowing that you made a promise to go to church too
It's funny how the people that mean you
no good you seek their advice
Didn't even think twice
Before you slept with that man
It's funny how you make time for him instead
of laboring in what would help you stand
Did you get the hint what I meant to say?
Is that it's funny how you can waste your day
Doing what!
Usually what you want chasing an endless hunt
That leads to nowhere
This message was meant to share

That behind the green I know your dark deeds

I know the deadly things you do to fulfill your needs

Yes, I'm Watching You

Remember I Created the Green Too!

I told you touch not the tree of the knowledge of good and evil

I told you to work

Darkness Is Coming Soon You Will Turn Back to Dirt

Stay alert

Watch and labor in that which was given unto you

Beyond The Green Lies Your Breakthrough

Set Your Soul Free

Give It All to Our Lord Almighty

See the vision write it plain claim it in Jesus' Matchless Name

Then water it and watch it grow

This Is the Answer to What You Want to Know

IT IS CONFIRMED CHILD GO!

The Word Is All About You

Can I Come Through?

I thought to myself,
What am I to say today?
You know, wanting to hear that one Word
that will redirect your sinful way
That will unite with Christ your obedience,
your discipline, and your self-control
That one Word that you claim made you whole
Well, here it is and it's true
That One Word is
YOU!
God said,
I told you to do something for Me which in
return will be for the benefit of you
So quick to jump around and claim your breakthrough
I told you too, to lose those men
To stop that habit which always leaves an opening for sin
I told you to build the vision, but with a turn of the dime
You changed your decision to do you
Once again you want to claim your breakthrough
I told you to keep the house clean

I told you that now is the time to birth that dream
I told you
Mr. and Mrs. Goodly too
To humble you!
I blessed you only to bless others

Your own pride

Got you on this ride

While you were supposed to be investing

in your sisters and brothers

That I placed under your care

I told you not to share

Your dreams with everybody

Because many around you are out to kill

You see, nobody likes to be left behind while you try to build

So, they hold you back

I told you not to trust all the facts

Because some people around you are trying to throw you off track

I told you to get to work

But when it's time to move you've got every

excuse to why it won't work

Or child I'm in pain life hurts

And you know what? It does. Life does hurt!

But can you just imagine an eternity in Heaven

When your body is returned back to dirt

I told you to stay alert

To watch and pray

I told you to read your bible faithfully every day

I told you to believe in you

Only then can My Word come through

I told you to do right by you

But what do you do?

You run,

You spend every day searching for fun

You talk,

Too afraid to walk out on faith

You live sinfully but continue to give Me thanks
You doubleminded man
You can't serve two masters and think one will help you stand
The devil, all he does is entice
Make wrong look right
Try to kill, steal, and rape your life
While God builds
God heals, God instills forever
Even in difficult times He keeps your pieces together
Unfailing love through all weather
Well, I hope you heard your Word and know exactly what to do
The one word is change you
For the better!
Now, thank God for this letter
This is that new day
Because you made up in your mind to live a new way
Stay true
No matter what or who follow through!
The Word Is All About You
You want more!
Get Honest Before the Lord!

The Process

I want you to hear what I have to say focus hard on these words
For, It Just Had To Be Heard

Living from wrong to right
Means sacrificing both the things you
love and transforming your life
It requires staying in the Word all day and night
It means praying for courage, wisdom, understanding, and sight
Let me break down this fight

I heard you say that you wanted to change
and walk into your destiny
I heard you pledge that you wanted to live to love only Me
But you fell short, turned around back into the
mess that I pulled you out of before
Why don't you give yourself a time to strive for more?
But you had every excuse
To why you couldn't put your actions to use
Always thinking, "I'll change, I'll start tomorrow"
But who told you that your tomorrow would come?
You can't run from Me my chosen one!

Many will ask
Yet only few will enter into the Paradise Land
Many have been called
Yet only few took the discipline to stand up
And release their stuck mentality to sin
I can't harvest your seeds until you allow my Holy Spirit in
Only then my child will you win!

It was Me, that allowed you to succeed in the midst of your storm
It was Me, that kept you sane and strong
I took what you treasured to find
That only I can build, instill, and kill what is needed for you to lead
It was me, yet why won't you completely believe
You can't love Me, and worship others
You can't place Me second to your sisters and brothers
How much pain do you want to endure?
For if you fail to faithfully obey, I will give you more
Until you surrender all
Everything you build will fall
Until you die to yourself
Every day you will live to serve someone else
Slave Mentality
Year after year living a lustful, prideful, and envious reality
What I laid down was not to be taken for granted
What I instill in you must be planted on this Earth
You too have options to live a curse or to live in your worth
Freedom of choice
Wasn't meant to destroy stop ignoring My voice!
Come! Put away your childish things and gain self-control
It's A Process
Yet, at the end you will be whole
Your soul
Will rise above the sky
Living not for less
Yet receiving only the best
Yet my Child you must begin

The Process!

I Will Rise!

I've been through a lot in my short life here on Earth
I've been kicked, stabbed, stoned, and covered in dirt
Yet still I rise
Keeping my mind focused on the prize
Giants I had to face
Setbacks I had to embrace
Yet can I be honest? I mean can I tell what's true?
As I grew into adulthood, I came to find
out that the true enemy is you

I see a frown
Let me break this down
As I walk through the valley of death
I have demons living in me
Crazy you see but I have to face reality
I have a lustful spirit
A restless spirit, procrastination, self-doubt, fear of failure,
Unorganized, low self-esteem, lack of patience,
Materialistic, priorities not in order
And I know all of this!

Yet. knowing and working to improve these areas
Requires discipline, courage, and strength
But every day I live I give thanks
Because it's another day to improve
Another day to walk amongst my enemies
And still move towards my prize
I thank God for one day
I WILL RISE!

Lord Touch Me in A Special Way

In the Name of Jesus Receive These Words That I Say

The Lord is my Shepherd
Why shall I want?
He fills my soul with joy
Allowing me to uplift our young girls and boys
He comforts me in times of distress
He cleanses me from my mess
He protects me from my enemies
Even the enemy that lives in me
He heals my wounds
Even through the storm I sing a praise tune
I call on the Name of the Lord
For I know that only with Him am I more
For His love is unfailing and His mercy endures forever
By faith I know that our spirits immerse together
Let every voice praise His Holy Name
Let The Great I Am be daily claimed
Let every knee bow before the Lord
For only through Him can we enter Heaven's Door
He is the Kings of all kings
He is the music of harmony in which my soul sings
Lord, please
Forgive me of all my sins
Allow Your Blood to wash me clean
I mean
I love you more than words can express
I confess,

I give thanks to You by following Your Commandments
I know that only for my protection were they sent
Let every day I live
Be a moment to give
Your teaching to those that pass my way
I love you Lord for who You are I pray never let me stray
From Your grace let me taste
The Fruits of the Spirit
Lord while I pray, I hope You hear it on this blessed day

LORD TOUCH ME IN A SPECIAL WAY

There's Healing Through The Storm

You just have to remember what doesn't
kill you makes you stronger
Stretch out your arms
To pull you out of the pit
Pay close attention for this was meant

Every one of you came from a different
story that placed you here
I'm sure that every one of you has a painful story to share
The question is what now do I do?
I say,
Plan and prepare for your breakthrough
First,
You have to forgive yourself
Release all the negative words told to you by someone else
Second,
You have to believe
That my setbacks and failures were
meant for me now to succeed
Yes!
We sometimes have to learn the hard way
We just didn't want to hear our warnings when others said
Slow Down!
But don't worry the truth shall be found
Thirdly,
You have to welcome good teachings in
It truly takes other positive people to help you win
Open your box that you so surely protect

Just think if you're stuck in one place then

how can you grow to the next

Level

Fourth,

And this one I'm going to keep it short but I must confess

Life changing ways is truly a process

You have to tell yourself daily that I deserve the best!

Stop settling for less

Give what it takes

In time you will notice a change in your fate

Fifth,

No more maybes or ifs

Accept Jesus as your Christ

Surrender all and watch how He directs your life

Six,

Learn to control

I tell you that denying your flesh, your lust, and your emotions

Will help make you whole

Seven,

You have to praise and give all glory to Heaven

Even through the good and bad

Even when you're sad or mad you have to give thanks

This completion will build your strength

It will keep you strong

I told you before

That

THERE'S HEALING THROUGH THE STORM!

A Living Sacrifice

When I just spoke these words, I couldn't
help but to see Jesus Christ
You see,
Because of Him I have life!

Oh man, how so quickly you are to quote a verse of the Bible
Of the Living Word
When you honestly know that you're not
living out all, which is heard!
You choose and pick what you are willing to obey
Knowing that I call you to move in all what I say
Like me,
You too must be willing to lay down your life each and everyday
I was not put on this Earth for me
I was granted life to bring others into their destiny
Laying hands on others while freeing the free
To follow is to be a daily responsibility
When you surely know that I can no longer live like this
I need you to pay attention for this you can't miss
What is being revealed is real
Lose that world from your spirit
Sound the alarm for I can hear it
You made it through
Your Breakthrough
Now my Son and Daughter you found you in Christ
For you chose to be
A Living Sacrifice

My Children Are Beginning to See!

That in these last days they must put all their faith in Me

The Almighty

Immanuel

Jesus known as Your Christ

I tell you it's a season of great change in Christians' lives

Old things are now cast away

This is a needed Word for a needed day

Heed what I say

It's a strange feeling that you feel

I mean the troubles that you embrace are real

You can't sleep

Your body feels weak

Where is your rest?

Why do you have so many worries upon your chest?

I confess

That it's through the storm

That you have no other choice but to cling to My arms

And it's true

In spite of I love the way you still praise yourself through

Now you're beginning to see

That I have a love for you that overpowers your daily reality

Be Still

And know that I Am God

Know that I will restore what the devil tried to rob

I am the Beginning and the End

So, stop worrying about your last day and start winning

Focus on things that are positive

On things that are good and worthwhile

Focus on things that are not of the wild
But things that are of Christ
Focus on empowering your soul and others' lives
Bow down on your knees
Confess to me saying Lord please
Have mercy on me
Lord live out your life through my body
Speak for me Walk with me
Claim me as your own
Son of God make my temple your home
Lord it's so true You fight for me!
Yes,
My Children Are Beginning to See!

Nothing Personal
But, Touch Me Not!

Stop

That wide opening for sin

If she is not your wife and you are not her husband

Sickness of your body will eventually come

Demons

Hunting you day and night

Nothing Personal but Touch Me Not

This Body belongs to Jesus Christ!

I apologize but now I realize

It's just not worth the hurt

You see, I know that there's life after our bodies return to dirt

Stay alert

Don't ignore the sign

Just watch the change

Slowly more and more slowly your sinful

familiar will seem distant and strange

Change for the better

God is always available through all kinds of weather

Lay it on the line

Do Right by You This Time

Let as I speak this issue drop

Nothing Personal

Man, but Touch Me Not!

And that's including yourself

Rapping your own body masturbating
to a fantasy or someone else
Let the truth be found
The time is now to get off the ground
And receive your crown
Dear King, Dear Queen
Go ahead and drop
Tell that sister or brother Nothing Personal but Touch Me Not!

Tell yourself for this is true
It's about time Soul that I do right by you
Resist the enemy and heed to these final words I drop

Touch Me Not!

Fighting Temptation

The damnation of this nation
Fighting for patience to win
Dying daily to sin!

My People
I too am human
I die daily to sin
Trying to live righteous yet these weaknesses hold me in
Then the same negative pattern begins
I too am human
I feel the pain
Those disappointing actions that brings yourself to shame
No one to blame but you denying what was true
I too am human
Living in the pit
Searching for a quick fix to bring happiness and self-worth
Seeking the true answer to why I was granted life on this Earth!
I too am human
No one seems to understand
The pressures that I experience on this land
This ongoing test
Winning yet still losing by choosing less
I too am human
Recognizing that the true enemy is me
Holding me back from making my dreams a reality
So, what should I do?
I too am human the same as you

**Fighting Temptation
The damnation of this nation
Fighting for patience to win
Dying daily to sin!**

Poem Inspired by Langston Hughes "I Too Am America"

This Is For You!

My Child
I understand that it's hard to come out of the wild
This season is one of loneliness, uncertainty, and despair
Where you look and nothing familiar is near
Yes! I do care!
But you have to go through
To bring out the best of you
Surrender, you see the more you fight the greater the pain,
Guilt, filth, and shame
Until you claim
Unshakably My Holy Name
Jesus Christ
I am the way to direct your life
My Daughter
My Son
You have all that it takes to build, to heal,
and to instill that which was given
My Chosen One
Don't just read but receive what is heard
Don't just listen but stand on My Word!
Yes!
It's true
That's why I said
This Is for You
My Child,
You are released from the wild
Move in My Name until all claim what's right
Jesus Christ
This Is Your Breakthrough
This Is For YOU!

Change Your Way Of Thinking!

I know what it's like to be addicted to something that kills
To be bounded by something that builds
Consuming more and more of you each day
You'd better heed what I say
One day it's got to go!
One day the effects of your wrongs will surely show!
You're no different from the next
So go and get your health check
What are you waiting for?
For sure, it seems like you have not yet learned the value of life
That's what happens when you're blinded from insight
When the Word doesn't direct your life
Now is, take this message and live
Child, love you more
There is no cure
You just have to stop
Drop! Your water pot and stop feeding
that which leads to a dead end
Stop dreaming of a new begin
And start moving, start believing, and
start achieving your goals
So let it be told
What you don't kill will surely kill you
I'm not talking to someone else I'm talking straight to you!
Do what is different from your daily routine!
You know what I mean

Change Your Way Of Thinking!

God
Ain't Nothing To Play With
Neither Is Your Time!

I apologize but the truth you must find

I never knew my worst enemy was me

So caught up that you overlook your true destiny

Do it

Get the job done

Stop playing my chosen one

For

Life is quick

Here one day then the next you're missed

Stop searching for a quick fix

And bring closure on that which needs to be closed

I chose

This just for you

You so close to your breakthrough

Who would have known

That it would be you

To speak for the Lord

To raise above and offering others more

But daily

I hope you hear me

Daily I watch you and I just can't understand

How you can place so much faith in man?

Without

Without certain things you feel incomplete

Then your actions manifest your self-defeat

Listen

Lift up your head

For you're being healed right now I said

What is to become shall surely be

God said that you can't run from your destiny

That there's many now living the same as me

Lost

Torn in between righteousness and fame

Obedience and the fast lane

I want you to make a decision

Me or fast living

Discipline or sinning

Remember, this isn't a game

We're talking about where your soul shall forever be claimed

Trust

It's well worth to die in God's Name it's for the benefit of us

Well

The time has come

I hope you're hearing my chosen one

For one day

You will be judged in the truth you find

GOD

AIN'T NOTHING TO PLAY WITH
NEITHER IS YOUR TIME!

Life or Death?

This Is A Promise Not A Threat

It's amazing how many fear the Earthly
consequences more than God
They confess for the fear of being robbed
Life
Their fear of being filled with pain, sorrow, misery, and strife
Their fear of those lonely nights
But oh, how so few
Fear for the righteousness of what the Word teaches you
If only man knew
That greater is He that is in him than he that is of this world
If only man knew how he can touch every
man, woman, boy, and girl
With God's Power
Healing after healing with each hour!
But so many are caught up trying to relieve some sin
That their true destiny doesn't even have a chance to begin
When?
When will you believe that you are next in kin?
To receive God's glory
Your life is His life story
But
So many only want to change when they feel bad
When they're tired of being mad
Faking happy but truly sad
What ever happened to changing in the good?
Like people succeeding in spite of the hood

Changing to only please God not yourself
Changing to honor the Great I Am not someone else
God
Knows your heart!
He knows your motives before you even start
Watch
Wait
And see
If you don't change for the better, you better believe
That like so many
Earthly consequences will come
Yes, upon all my chosen one
But,
What is to come surely it's ten times greater
than these Earthly consequences
Child this is about your soul!
Who
Heaven or Hell shall hold?
For eternity
I hope you hear me
For the time has come
Make A Decision My Chosen One

This is a promise not a threat!
Make your choice
Life or Death?

Talk to My Children About
Running This Rat Race

Promises of riches and happiness if you could only get to that place

Not knowing that it's an endless chase

Because you will always want more

Where will you be satisfied for sure?

There is one thing certainly deeper than money

In Heaven for eternity flowing in milk and honey

And God adds no sorrow to it

Pay close attention for this was meant!

You are more than materialistic things

You are more than praying for a wedding ring

Stop comparing to your neighbors

Stop living all day and night in labor

The race is not giving to the swift but to the one that endures

Appreciate what you have, focus on the good, and

give thanks to God for blessing you with more

More love, faith, hope, mercy, joy, forgiveness, good health,

abundancy, God's life and word, and His unfailing grace!

Only with Jesus Do We Win This Race!

He said that I am going to prepare a place for you

and when all is ready I will come and get you so

that you will always be with me where I AM

For I AM the way, the truth, and the life

No one can come to the Father except through me

Lord of Heaven's armies Jesus your Christ

Just believe that I am in the Father and the Father is in me or

at least believe because of the work you have seen me do

I tell you what is true

Anyone who believes in me will do the same works, I have

done, and even greater works, because I AM going to be

with the Father. You can ask for anything in My Name,

and I will do it, so that the Son can bring glory to God

Returning an unlimited fold of what the enemy robbed

Jesus said, "that I am leaving you with a

gift-peace of mind and heart

And the peace I give is a gift the world cannot give

So don't be troubled or afraid abundantly live

Remember, the ruler of this world has no power over me

Yet I did what the Father required of me

And sacrificed my body

So that the world will know that I love

the Father come let's be going

Let the glory of God be showing

For when you produce much fruit, you are my true disciples

for this brings great glory to our Father from above

This I command from each other is to love

The Holy Spirit of Truth our Advocate sent by Jesus himself

Will guide us into our better selves

For he will tell us whatever he receives from Jesus

In his Matchless Name do trust

That if God is for us who or what can be against us

Smile and be glad and celebrate when others succeed

Even if they are in the lead

In God still praise and believe

That our time to shine shall come

My Chosen One

It requires work

To build greatness out of dirt
Just speak whatever is needed in my Name
In Jesus do claim
For at the end of the day when you are put
into your final resting place
All the things you acquired on Earth won't matter in
Eternity just remember that as you run this rat race
Now as I requested from the writer above
I too have a request from you my love
In these words, do heed and fully embrace!

Talk to My Children About Running This Rat Race!

Nothing Is Perfect
But GOD!

You just have to be honest with yourself
If you feel the need to be with someone else
then you need to be by yourself
Don't be selfish
What doesn't move only holds back!
Don't deny the facts
And don't settle for one day your true desire will manifest
While others are hurt because you can't live with less

Take this brief moment to appreciate
The beauty of life Child you are not too late
You're just on time
Trust the truth you will find
Just make a small change
To make what was so familiar feel strange
Just do something that you've never done before
Fall to the floor
And ask for forgiveness
Ask for your shame to be removed
For your sin to be washed
For your guilt to be erased
Fall on your face
And
Humble yourself my Child
It takes great courage to come from amongst the wild

But,
Don't be so hard on yourself
Don't allow the devil to rob!
Just speak

Nothing
Is Perfect
But
GOD!

I Am
What The Word Says
I Am

I AM
A Child of God

Jehovah
Yahweh
Hosanna of the Highest

I AM
Healed by Jesus Christ's stripes
I AM
Living a fruitful life
I AM
Blessed for my obedience to the Word
I AM
Able to understand and put in action the
true meaning of what is heard
I AM
A new creature unlike others
I love my enemies and all my sisters and brothers
When I walk many witness the Robe of God covering me
They envy my favor and anointing you see
I was conceived
To believe
To build thou Kingdom Come on Earth
I AM

Saved by God's grace which taught me my worth

I AM

All power for the Word lives in me

I AM

Unstoppable making my dreams a reality

I AM

Me

Too blessed to be stressed

Too faithful for settling for less

As I raise

I will continue to give Heaven praise

As I ascend

I will continue to lift up all children, women, and men

Why?

I AM What the WORD Says I AM

I was born to stand and to trudge over satan's deadly trap

By God's Blood I AM soaring throughout this land

Tell me, where do you stand?

Did you hear what was heard?

I AM What the WORD Says I AM

MY CHILD the answer is in the

WORD!

I Boldly Call Forth!

In Jesus the Son of God's Name the
Throne of Our Gracious God
To Receive His Mercy to Find Grace
Holy Spirit Fill This Place
Our High Priest Intercede as I Plead My Case

I begin
By first asking for forgiveness of my sins
When
I failed to follow through
The will You
Had for me
I never knew that I was my worst enemy
The enemy in me
But whatsoever came I continued to trust
"If God is for us, who can ever be against us?"

I next will raise up Your Holy Name
The Great I Am the One and Only True God to Claim
How great thou are
Creator of all things shining from here to afar
The glue that pieces all together
"His faithful love endures forever!"

This is what I speak
I call forth the power to bind the devil
and to strengthen what is weak
"For I have the authority

Over all the power of the enemy"

Even the one in me

I call forth prosperity

To build thou Kingdom Come

To give love to everyone

For

"Both Gentiles and Jews

Who believe the Good News

Share equally in the riches inherited by God's children"

So Let It Be Done

I call forth that the world knows that I Am God's Chosen One

"Who dares accuse us whom God has chosen for his own?

No one for God himself has given us right standing with himself"

I call forth the fruits of the Spirit to

transform me to my better self

I Plead

For the skilled ability to lead

With wisdom, understanding, charity, faith, and love

Laboring only for the glory of above

For in this I wholeheartedly trust

"Overwhelming victory is ours through Christ, who loved us"

I boldly call forth that my life works God will say well done

That I have believed and done my best

"For only we who believe can enter his rest"

I Am

A Friend of God

I Am

You and you are me

I call forth oneness now with the Holy Trinity

May my husband be blessed

May my children be blessed

May my family be blessed

May my enemies be blessed

May my health be blessed

May my mind be blessed

May my soul be blessed

May my body be blessed

May all Heaven be blessed

May this Earth be blessed

With your mercy

May we all find your grace

As I plead my case

At home

As I speak before Your Throne

I boldly call forth that Christ decree

"Because you believed,

It has happened"

Surely it shall come

My Chosen One

I shout to the east, west, to the south, and north!

The Power of God

I Boldly Call Forth!

I Understand

You see, I too became man
I know about the constant choices
I know about ignoring your inner voices
That warn you from harm
I know about wanting to cry in someone's arm
Searching for answers trying to sustain
Sinning yet still calling on my name
I know what it's like to claim
Defeat
Surrounded by the negativity on the streets
I too was a man
I know about wishing for true love on this land
Slaving for a high
Living a lie
Praying every day to die
To sin
When
Will you realize?
That I too cry
Why!
Why can't man see?
That greater is He
That dwells within you than he that is of this world
That death comes upon every man, woman, boy, and girl
Change your way of thinking!
Start believing in you
I understand
What it's like to be so close to your breakthrough

Yes
I confess
That your time has come
To do the impossible my chosen one
Stand
Go to a mirror and say
That today is the day
To make what is not so
Go
Move and not think
Don't worry your health and your strength will not faint
I too had to make a decision
For whom I'm living
Heaven or hell
I tell
You no lie
I too was man!
Whatever you experience

I Understand

My Son

Pull Yourself Together, Unleash Your Inner Strength

Allow Your Light to Shine Through!

You Were Created in My Image

Now, You Must Live as I Commanded You To!

Until You Take Control Over Your Life

I Will Not Bless You with Your Wife

Until You Believe

I Will Not Grant You What You Want

Or So Desperately Need

You Must Come Through Me

In Order to Succeed!

Let Us Explore,

Reaching for Your Inner Core

MY SON,

You Must Sacrifice Yourself in Order to Achieve More!

Stop Chasing! Stop Wasting!

Your Time!

Be Patient,

THE TRUTH YOU SHALL FIND!

MY SON

My
Daughter

I watch you from below
I see your will to grow
Yet,
You are stuck for you have failed to let go!
This you must know!
Your King doesn't destroy your Spirit
He doesn't vex your Soul
He doesn't put you down
Yet, He builds to make you whole!
Stop Chasing Pain!
Stop giving of yourself
When there's nothing to gain!
Love You!
Love Everything that makes you
You!
It's your lack of love for self
That keeps you down and blue
I told you what you needed to hear
Yet, you failed to believe in yourself
You really didn't try!
You know it too
That's why on the inside you cry!
Yes, there's many to do
Yet,
Pace yourself it will eventually be through
I Told You My Daughter

To Love Yourself as I Do for You
Don't Think! Just Do!
NOW MOVE!

My

Daughter

Prayer Is The Stairway To Heaven

Therefore, We Speak

Almighty GOD please listen down from Your Seat

And be merciful to our prayers

For scripture says, *to cast our cares*

Unto You

We declare that Your Power come through

That the Holy Spirit that lives in You

Fall down unto us

For in Jesus Christ Son of God we do trust

I thank you Father for this day

For Your breath of life

That woke me up this morning and started me on my way

I am not worthy, yet You still claim me as your own

In Heaven you have prepared my home

I know that I'm not alone

For with every decision, I can hear your tone

Guiding me, protecting me, restoring me

Even from me!

I say,

May this day bring you the greatest glory

May I live out the Word of your Good Story

May I grow

May Your anointing show

May I move in favor

May I love all even my worst enemies and neighbors

May I find a peace

Time to share with You my Savior on the Word's great feast

May my pressures be release

May I labor for my Father's Will

May old wounds be healed

May my health be well and whole

May I receive nourishment for my Soul

So let it be true

So let it be done unto you

For scripture says, *seek Me first and all*
these things shall be added unto you

God said that My Word is Forever True!

THEREFORE, WE SPEAK

Almighty GOD please listen down from Your Seat

Amen

With You Christ Jesus it's always a win-win!

Ask and Turn

This you will learn

I didn't come here for everyone
I came here for you
This is your word can I come through
You see,
First you have to welcome me
Into your heart
In order for your salvation to start
You have to unshakably believe
That this is my Word, and I shall receive

You know,
I researched prayer and found a scripture from Acts 3:19
Now pay close attention this isn't as easy as it seems
The scripture said
Ask Jesus to forgive you of your sins and make you new in Him
Now turn from your sins and turn to God,
so you can be cleansed of your sins
This is where the hard process begins
Now turn
This is the area in which so many burn!
Where so many failed to learn
Self-discipline
Self-control
This is the process in which you grow to become whole
It is there
That you have to address your worst fears

Where you have to lose what you grew to care

For

It is there where you have to decide that I want more

That I love me more

That I have to conquer this inner war

Roaring in me

You know,

It's hard to defeat sin when it became your daily reality

So, what do you do?

The word said, now turn from your sins

and turn to God to break through

It says so you can be cleansed of your sins

Don't you understand that you have to release

in order for the new you in Him to begin!

I know what it's like to be controlled by something or someone

I know what it's like to wait before the dream has begun

Surrounded by others yet still alone

Compromising your morals your values in order to not be alone

Trying to maintain your home

No

It's not easy and we all have something

or someone that we run to

To help us get through

But,

God said that is what I'm supposed to do

Come before Me in prayer and I shall come into you

I have a comfort that no man can give

I have a love that will always live

I have a mercy and grace

That will fill your space

With joy and laughter

With peace

It is at this time that I am creating for you a great feast

So be still and know that I Am God

It is only I that shall never leave

Believe

What I say

God is creating for you a new day

Yet,

It requires work

It requires energy

It requires movement

Pay attention for this is it, this is what you came here to learn!

It requires you to

Ask & Turn

I Want to Talk about Follow-Through

The last part of your break-through
Requires you to follow-through
Let us examine this word
I need you to accept what is heard
In order to change
The title of this sermon of this poem is

Living in the Strange

Requires a great cost
This is where so many souls are lost
Caught in between
It required great obedience that you found
out is not as easy as it seems
You have to admit that you have a problem
You have to embrace the facts
You have to get back on track
And push through
This word is just for you

What is the problem?
I told the Lord me
He said the problem is that you're caught in between destiny
I know you hear me
I speak to you everyday
You know what is wrong you know
what to do heed to what I say
But you're so confused

So caught up in mess
So used to living in less
That you can't see
That the love of your dreams can be a reality
Love doesn't hurt trust me

You love it more than you love yourself
You have not learned to appreciate you but
only finding purpose in someone else
But what about you?
What about laboring hard to make your inner
desire your destiny your very being come true
But you're covered in so much sin you can't
even see your own way through
Didn't you hear the word?

Follow-Through

What is the first word Follow!
Follow who?
It's during this process that your actions
speak who you gave your alliance to
Which road are you traveling have you
even slowed down to see?
That am I living in the purpose that my
Father that my God created for me?
Be still
Stop don't make a decision until you
know for sure that this is real
How can you love others when you
truly honestly don't love you?
How can you break through?

With baggage holding you down
I tell you that for you the truth has been found
This is what you were waiting to hear
This is why I'm up here to share
And it's true
God has His hand on you!
In spite of yourself you will make it through!
But you have to make one move and God
shall supply all your needs
You have to believe
That this came just for you!
God said
Child

Follow-Through!
Follow Me and you will make it through
The ultimate place is Heaven that you are trying to make it into
Follow Me and I will direct you
For at this time you can't see
Where to go and how to bring forth your true destiny
So allow Me to lead
And you shall succeed
Yes
You
Not another wasted day do what you know what to do
Go
Follow-(Him) Through!

Chapter 2
IF GOD KEPT YOU THUS FAR!

"God didn't bring you this far to leave you." (Philippians 1:6)

"Believe in the Lord Jesus, and you will be saved,
you and your household." (Acts 16:31)

"God, your God, will restore everything you lost; he'll have compassion
on you; he'll come back and pick up the pieces from all the places
where you were scattered. No matter how far away you end up, God,
your God, will get you out of there." (Deuteronomy 30: 3-4).

If God Kept Me Thus Far

Then why should I worry about the future plan?
If I survived thus far then I will continue
to place my faith in God's hand
I understand
That I am only a man
God controls all
Down to my success and to my downfalls
Victory is mine!
My life is led by the Holy Spirit so there is no waste of time
Everything happens for a reason
There are all different types of seasons
That one must go through
And I don't know about you
But I am counting on the Lord for my breakthrough
I'm not saying that it's easy in fact it requires a great cost
But through it all I know that without
Jesus Christ I would be lost
There were many nights I had to say Father take my hand
And help me stand
On my own
Father make my problems your own
I give them unto you
For only Father do you know what to do
I tell you
I humbled myself under God
For these Earthly treasures the devil can rob
By what God gives
Makes all man live

In a silent peace

An assurance that you will not embrace defeat

So, go ahead and praise

Before God rise your feeble legs

Go ahead and give thanks

Before God renews your strength

You feel it the victory is here

I just came to confirm and share

That it is finished it is complete!

It is healed and made whole!

So let it be told

That you can't reach a star

But it's still there you see it from afar

So why lose faith

If God Kept You Thus Far!

Come and Grow!

I'm Not Going to Tell You What You Want to Hear
I didn't come here to share
A fantasy
You hear me
I'm going To Tell You What You Need To Know
To grow

"How long will you fools hate knowledge" (Proverbs 1:22)
I'm not talking about the education
that you receive from college
I'm talking about conquering that sin
I'm talking about what you allow your eyes to let in
To your soul
There are so many of you praying to be made whole
But refuse to surrender and be led
God said
"When they cry for help, I will not answer.
Though they anxiously search for me, they
will not find me (Proverbs 1:28)
You see,
"They hated knowledge and chose not to
fear the Lord" (Proverbs 1:29)
Always yearning for more
"They rejected my advice and paid no attention
when I corrected them (Proverbs 1:30)
Placing her and him
Before Me

Working to obtain, claim, and maintain
things became your reality
"Therefore, they must eat the bitter fruit of living their own
way, choking on their own schemes" (Proverbs 1:31)
And you said that you had a dream
To fulfill
Areas in your life that you wanted healed
My Chosen One
"I called you so often, but you wouldn't come" (Proverbs 1:24)
And it hurts
That we couldn't build oneness before you returned back to dirt
Need I mention?
"I reached out to you, but you paid no attention." (Proverbs 1:24)
"You ignored my advice." (Proverbs 1:25)
And now you sit here troubled over life

I pleaded before God with the support of Jesus Christ
While led I said
Father what do we do?
When we are tired faking that we have our breakthrough?
He answered,
For a fact
Know that
Greater is He (Christ) that is in you than
he (man) that is of this world
Everything you need to know to grow my
dear man, woman, boy, and girl
Is in the Word
Read it for yourself and live out what is heard
I'm Coming Through

It's true

God said I'm waiting on you

Come

My Chosen One

The Altar Is Open

I'm hoping

You don't ignore my call once again

This time I came in person

In front of you to tell and to show

I'm Not Going to Tell You What You Want to Hear

I'm Going to Tell You What You Need to Know

Now is

Come and Grow!

Like action there is a verb

Wisdom Is Calling In Proverbs

Go home and read

You will find your Word

Believe

Amen

So let it be done

Today God Is Uplifting His Chosen One

This you must know!

Come to the Altar and Grow!

Be Encouraged My Chosen One

Speak right now to yourself and know that change has come
I'm speaking to all God's chosen ones
I know that trouble has surrounded you
But with each trial somehow you made it through
I know that death has swept through our nation
That your need for money has left you impatient
I know
That your desire for true love seems to hurt more than to grow
To all those that feel weak I speak this you must know
Homeless people be encouraged for you shall be sheltered
Starving people be encouraged for you shall be filled
Sick people be encouraged for you shall be healed
Addicts be encouraged for your addiction shall be killed
All people know that this is real
In this time of trouble, lean so ever forward on God
In this time of trouble, the devil is trying to rob
Your joy, your peace, your sleep
Your rest, Your release of stress
Your home
Your family
Your own
Body
He is trying to steal your mind your time
Your soul's forever resting place
At this time be still and embrace
The Goodness of God
Surrender All
For I promise that to trust in Jesus, Son of God you will not fall

Hold on

Speak the Word of God to keep you strong

Meditate

Allow the stillness of God to overcome your fate

I had to know

That I will not die I will live and grow

That the Lord is my strength and my

song He has given me victory!

For my life is my Savior's life story!

That this is the day the Lord has made

we will rejoice and be glad in it

Child of God this is meant

Give thanks to the Lord, for He is good and

His faithful love endures forever

Let us stand up in victory together

For change has come!

Be Encouraged My Chosen One!

Stop Doubting Yourself!

I don't know about you but allow me to minister to myself
When I think of doubt, I see an unstable person
And when I think of an unstable person
I see the Word "A double-minded man
is unstable in all his ways"
You'd better pay attention to the Word on this page
For it's true
You say one thing and then the next you doubt you
And other word you don't follow-through
I know so now what do you do?
Shake off all that dirt
And work!
I don't care if you have to work from sunrise to sunset
Labor hard Child to get your goals met
For this one life is short here today then gone the next
Stop worrying about everyone else and get yourself in check
Oh, I'm thanking God that we met
For what is to come unto you
Child if you would just labor for the right
thing what a blessing that awaits you
Doing what you were truly called to
Well, I think that's enough of beating up on you
For even after I speak I bet you still continue to do you
What is it going to take?
To make
You see
That greater is the God in me
He shall have His way

Even if you have to pay
For your disobedience
You're no better than someone else!
If you want to live than

Stop Doubting Yourself!

It's Time!

My Lord and Savior
Come upon me with great favor
This is for you my dear neighbor

My eyes are opened to the truth
May these words by the grace of God inspire you to

I was raised by society to believe
That I had to possess man-made standards in order to succeed
And I was trained wrong!
You see,
The Lord doesn't care about our materialistic
things in the midst of His storm!
I say His storm for this life we live is truly war
For sure,
Hell, and Satan are real
Their whole purpose for living is to kill
what has been instilled within you
I need you to hear what I'm saying for it's true
God has His mighty hands on you!

I couldn't see,
I thought that I needed the marriage,
the great career, the family,
The house, and the cars
To be living and striving to be all I can be
How wrong was the childish thinking that lived in me!
It's about the Souls!

It's about giving of yourself to make others become whole!
It's about the Word of God being taught to the entire nation
It's about living daily with love, understanding,
forgiveness, and great patience!
It's about you
Growing into what the Lord created for you to do!

I questioned myself, who am I to speak?
Lord when there are still so many areas in me that are weak
Areas that need to grow areas in me that I need to let go!
But,
I serve a God that is able to heal, able to build, and instill
His Holy Will in me
He said, I chose you in spite of your everyday reality!
I chose you in spite of your sins
He said, this is why I died so that you may be able to live again!
The question is, when?
When are you going to receive His merciful grace?
When are you going to withdraw from
this man-made hell race?
When are you going to see the truth?
Your time is few
My Child God Told Me To Tell You
That it's time to receive the greatest blessing that I gave!
It's your time
My Child
To Be
SAVED!

I Shall Not Be Moved!

Curse me, hate me, and put me down
I still will wear my anointed crown!
You see,
I'm a survivor there is no stopping me!
All things are done through Christ and
I know what I have a right to
You just can't seem to understand
That I was granted dominion and authority amongst this land!
Fear, is not a word I claim
I don't need riches and fame
To feel my strength
I tell you what all I have to do is give thanks
So, go ahead plan all your vicious attacks
Pull out all your lethal weapons
Stab me in the back
I dare you to try to throw me off track
I will not be moved
I guess soon
You'll discover that fact
Laugh
I'll still walk with my head up high
You see,
I'll still claim Jesus even after I die
I'll tell you what,
You might as well join my righteous groove!
Because I told you before

I Shall Not Be Moved!

I Smile

And praise my Savior

For blessing me with abundant favor

Every time you curse my name

I smile for my Lord had to adore the same

Lies

With each nasty word my destiny is

fulfilled I don't crumble I rise

What Earthly things can you take?

It is not my job title or materialistic things that mold my fate

I smile

At my struggles, trials, and when my enemies awake

I'm too blessed to be stressed

I know when the storm comes I'm at my best

My Savior fights for me so defeat I could never confess

Throw dirt

I'll smile

Kick me where it hurts

I'll smile

Bring up my past filled with shame and guilt

I'll smile

Why? Because I'll still be here able to speak

and make perfect what's wrong

Why? Because I know that this test won't last long

Why? Because I am a Child of God

where no man is above Him!

Why? Because I was born to win

I Smile

At evil and foolish sin!

I recognize
The devil lies
I know my worth
And as long as I live I will continue to smile on this Earth
Saving all my sisters and brothers
Making peace amongst one another
I live to win
Loving my Lord while denying sin
Everlasting Lord let Your Holy Spirit dwell within
Amen

I Smile!

Greater is God!

I plead the Blood of Jesus overall which was robbed, from me

Devil you can't destroy, steal, kill, take, or

hinder what God wrote for my destiny

I will love and be loved by our God Almighty!

FatherGodSpirit,

I thank you all day and night

I pray Lord help me appreciate life

And not take for granted

Not be troubled by childish matters when Your

Will here on this Earth must be planted

As I grow more and more in one with You!

My Father, I get it, I AM to unfailingly trust in You through

all my trials and tribulations transitions and breakthroughs!

I SMILE

Sharing my learnings

Making God first in all things connected to my life

I love and forgive as commanded from above

Letting go of negativity, weaknesses of the flesh, and strife

Eternity in Heaven with God is my final flight

So, I Am blessed coming in even being born

And blessed going out even in death

So, I laugh at your vicious words, actions, and vindictive threats

For I have a peace that surpasses all man's

understanding a joy that only God could give

A trust that God is always with us and an

inheritance that Satan tried to rob!

But victory in all these things I shall see for

Greater is God!

Push Through

Even through the storm God said, "I got you!"
For through My Blood
My Children I granted you My unfailing love
Like a butterfly in its cocoon
Soon you too shall arise with your beautiful wings
Praising God for the new song that you are able to sing
My grace is sufficient, for my strength is
made perfect in your weakness
I need you to peep this
God goes before you clearing the way to fulfill His Will
For you on this Earth
Now is, you are living in your true worth
Creating greatness out of dirt
Stay alert, for greater is God than he or it of this world
Carry this message all men, women, boys, and girls
That God is here amongst us
In Him, only do we trust
So, when trouble comes with confidence
we speak victory over me and you!
For with God on our side we were destined to

PUSH THROUGH!

I told you before God said, "I got you!"
Smile and PUSH THROUGH
Persevere Under Stress Harmoniously Take Hear
Rest On the Unfailing word of God to Heart
This is your new start!

Through The Blood of
JESUS CHRIST!

I pray Holy Spirit come upon me as I write
For, A WORD is needed at this time
I pray may a personal relationship with Jesus our Lord
and Savior you right now all receive, retrieve, and find
In Jesus' Matchless Name Amen
FatherGodSpirit let the truth begin
For We Were Born to WIN!
So, do know that God is greater than our reality, our
trials, our successes, our downfalls, and our sin!
I pray live these Words from Our Beginning and Our End
My Children when
The storm rages now is the time to move by faith
To know already that you will be kept safe
in advance giving God thanks
For, the BLOOD of JESUS CHRIST saved our lives
He made the crooked way straight, the dead
end an opening, and all wrongs right
Therefore, no weapon formed against us shall prosper and
greater is He that lives in us than he or it that lives in this world
I SPEAK
Together as one we shall praise God shouting
"Glory" yes, all men, women, boys, and girls
For, it took our one praise
To defeat the devil bruising his head, feet, crippling his legs
For We Are Children of God

In this Due Season we retrieve what
was killed, stolen, and robbed
Yes, we rise up
We break through, overcome, and conquer what was
dormant, chained, tied up, blocked, and stuck
Enough is Enough!
We will embrace all change with a confident peace
That none of these things will come close to my feet,
to my home, to my family, to all connected to me
May God right now release
A peace that surpasses all man's understanding and may
you smile, be filled with joy and a great assurance that
this too shall pass God said that my grace is sufficient
for you, for my power is made perfect in weakness
Just look around and peep this
Do not touch my anointed ones; do my prophets no harm
So, no need to be alarmed!
God just said that I got you in the shelter
and the strength of His arms
Abba, our Daddy
We now praise you
For all you continue to say, move on, and do
We are nothing but a breath of air without you
Father, we love you, we trust in you, and we glorify you
Almighty Creator
Our way maker
We thank you in advance for the victory for the light at the
end of the tunnel, for making us the salt of this world
Pass this on to every man, woman, boy, and girl

And do share that Jesus came that we
might live abundantly in this life
Therefore, we now throw out all that does not belong, all that
kills, steals, robs, Lord we give to you now all our strife!
And we receive now our victory

Through the Blood of JESUS CHRIST!

Amen! I told you before that we were born to win!

Who Do You Love More?

The LORD or Yourself?
The ways of the truth or pleasing someone else?
This story affects the lives of many today
For we are caught up in our own selfish ways
Pay close attention to what I say

It took a real shaking in my life
For me to realize that my daily living
was not pleasing in God's sight
That I found more pleasure in wrong than right
The process to victory is not an easy task
Some tests are learned quickly while
others seem too forever last
Do you want to know the weapons that
are formed against you to fail?
What Satan uses to capture so many Souls in Hell?

Your Weakness of the Flesh
Your own desire to satisfy that need
Satan deceiving you to believe
That it will fulfill
Sinning in God's sight while praying
to be delivered and healed!

For Sure
Tell Me
Who Do You Love More?

Your Eyes
Lusting for what they see
Your *eyes* are the source which controls your destiny
Pleasing in your sight
Just a glance made you forget how you
were commanded to live right
Allowing Satan victory that night!

Which King lies on the other side of the door?
Tell me,
Who Do You Love More?

Your Pride
If you weren't acknowledged properly
you thought, you would die
Craving for first
All the worldly treasures you unchangeably thirsted for
Partaking in Satan's deadly curse
More
More
Did you ever think when will enough be
enough when will I ever be satisfied?
Tell me
Who Do You Love More?
For
With Satan you are destined to die
Who Do You Love More?
Stop living a lie
Running
Wasting

Chasing
A test that will always fail
Who Do You Love More?
Stop dying for Hell!

My Child
This is not a game
I'm not blessing you with these words for power or fame
This is real
Do You Love Me?
Then stop letting Satan steal what I instilled in you
Who Do You Love More?
Stay True!
Because if you loved me then you would do right by
You!

Touch Me in A Special Way

In the Name of Jesus Receive These Words That I Say

The Lord is my Shepherd
Why shall I want?
He fills my soul with joy
Allowing me to uplift our young girls and boys
He comforts me in times of distress
He cleanses me from my mess
He protects me from my enemies
Even the enemy that lives in me
He heals my wounds
Even through the storm I sing a praise tune
I call on the Name of the Lord
For I know that only with Him am I more
For His love is unfailing and His mercy endures forever
By faith I know that our Spirits immerse together
Let every voice praise His Holy Name
Let The Great I Am be daily claimed
Let every knee bow before the Lord
For only through Him can we enter Heaven's Door
He is the Kings of all kings
He is the music of harmony in which my soul sings
Lord, please
Forgive me of all my sins
Allow Your Blood to wash me clean
I mean
I love you more than words can express
I confess,

I give thanks to You by following Your Commandments
I know that only for my protection were they sent
Let every day I live
Be a moment to give
Your teachings to those that pass my way
I love you Lord for who You are I pray never let me stray
From Your grace let me taste
The Fruits of the Spirit
Lord while I pray, I hope You hear it on this blessed day
LORD TOUCH ME IN A SPECIAL WAY
AMEN!

The Turn Of The Century Has Come!

Where those that praise the Name of

Jesus shall be united as one

Overflow of blessings has begun

Those that were looked over are now viewed as someone

My Child

You are growing

Your anointed gifts that were deferred are showing

Shining bright amongst this world

No more childish thinking no more little boy and girl

You stand bold in My Name

Even when against the rule you are willing to claim

You surrendered

You welcomed Me into your Soul

You labored faithfully to maintain balance

and make what was empty whole

You know it too

Many are just starting to recognize

the real you coming through

Many days

You prayed

Unto Me for guidance, strength, and wise insight

Many days you sacrificed

So that others may have and believe in Me

The time has come to release back what you have done daily

Trust

I know your heart

I knew the glory that I would receive from you from the start

Smile

And watch your obedience pay
Receive what is written and the words that I say

The World Shall Know You As My Chosen One
So let it be written
So let it be done
THE TURN OF YOUR CENTURY HAS COME!

To All My House Builders

TO ALL MY HARVEST INSTILLERS
Hear what is from TRUE
This message was sent just for you!

You want to build thou Kingdom Come on Earth
Then you must build what I have placed in your care
You must be willing to share
Your financial gifts
No more maybes or ifs
You must sow into all who were chosen as My Children
Or no matter what you're preaching and
teaching will still keep them in the wild
Stop!
Building up fine buildings and start building your church!
The church is the people
The temple lies within them
It's time to win
And let Heaven on Earth come
Hell shall cease
I'm calling out all my preachers from
the north, south, west, and east
Let that spirit release
Let Hell claim defeat
Let us heal!
Let us instill
Trust!

This was not meant for all but sent to us
To God's Healers
This message is meant
To All My House Builders
Don't hate the Messenger, do not dare to hate the message
For this is true
Like all God shall judge you too!
House Builders
To my so-called Harvest Instillers
Hear what is true
This message was sent just for you!

BUILD!
FOR GOD'S WILL!

Can These Old Bones Live Again?

I tell you,

When I was in my prime

Child, your grandmother was sharp as a dime

So many men hoping to find a life with me

I swore then that I was going to live out my destiny

Child, I was going to birth my dreams

But, I quickly found out that it wasn't as easy as it seems

Life kicks in

So many trials and tribulations

That your goals are put on hold before

they even have a chance to begin

Then,

Don't have a giving heart

Got so many people around trying to help

them once again you prolong your start

So, what do you do?

Usually, you give up your dreams and

start working for the man too

So many wasted days

Watching your health fade

And still not fulfilling your goals

Tell me can these dry bones

Live again

Is there still time to win?

The Lord Speaks

If you're still breathing then you still have

time to strengthen what is weak

I told you before to seek

The Kingdom of Heaven and all its righteous to win
Only then
Will you live in your true worth!
The answer is yes!
Right now, make your difference of this Earth
Work
Labor
Move
In spite of deny sin!
Yes!

Your Old Bones Will Live Again!

Let These Words I Claim

When I was a child
I thought as a child
I behaved as a child
I spoke as a child
But,
When I became an Adult, I put away childish things

Let these words I claim in Jesus Name

Every day I will read Your Word
I will live out the wisdom that I heard
I will die daily to my sinful ways
I will make the most out of each day
I will humble myself
I will care for the weak and encourage someone else
I will serve
I will give all the love that they deserve
I will preach
I will teach the Good News to all who yearn to hear
I will not live in self-doubt, worry, and fear
I will care
For the needy
I will shelter
The homeless and enlighten the lost
Every day I will praise the Lord for He
first paid the ultimate cost
For me
I will live holy

I will labor to make Heaven here on Earth a reality
I will
Because the Word says that I put away all childish things
I became an adult so that my Lord's
Spirit can dwell in me and bring
What Heaven
Overflows with from above!
I
Surrendered
To

LOVE!

IN JESUS' NAME
LET THESE WORDS I CLAIM

Are You Ready To Win?

This is the season the moment of change

Where what was once familiar seems strange

And the new you seem so far away

But,

This is the new day

Now we are going to discuss some side effects of this season

Trust, if you're listening to this it's for a reason

I see a frown

Let me break this down

First,

To break this curse

You have to know what you want

Remember there's a season to plant, to gather, and to hunt

Second,

I must share

Prepare!

Every good enemy spies out his opponent

studying him or her at work and at rest

Remember with every sin you must confess

Third,

I know that this is constantly heard

Move immediately don't hold back

Remember you have to block the negative opinions

Even family from pushing you off track

Fourth,

This one is real short

Stand your ground

Remember watch and be aware of all sounds

For the enemy will attack it's a proven fact

Remember, don't allow people to steal your joy

But you stay in control of what you say and how you react

Fifth,

This one you can't miss

Forgive yourself for mistakes you will make

But remember if you follow these rules

you will redirect your fate!

Remember, it's never too late to do something

different to change your life

Sixth,

Turn it all over to Jesus Christ

Surrender tonight this is your confirmation to do right!

Amen!

Seventh,

ARE YOU READY TO WIN?

My Daily Pledge

Today,
I pledge to love myself a new way
To only speak positive words
To take in all the wisdom that I heard

Today,
I understand that no one is perfect we all make mistakes
Yet,
Those that achieve labored to redirect their fate
I shall succeed for I believe in me
Strong, intelligent, and eager to make my dreams a reality

Today,
I will acknowledge the special people in my life
I will show appreciation to all those
who stress to guide me right
I will keep my sight on Christ

Today,
I will renew myself
Taking time out just for me and nobody else
Exploring my talents and sharing with others
Loving all my enemies and sisters and brothers

Today,
My health is well
My mind is sane
My spirit is filled

My hands are anointed to heal
My soul anointed to build and instill our future leaders

Today,
I am a believer
I hold the key

Today,

I AM

SO PROUD OF ME!

I Changed My Speech

I stop speaking from an area focusing not on perfection
but dwelling on that which keeps you weak
I stop saying what I can't have
What is not meant for me to grab
And I just did it!
I mean finishing up on those goals that were meant!
And I moved!
I got in a Holy-Ghost groove!
Birthing all things that were destined for me to produce
I stop talking about things that add no use
To my vision
I stop watching television
And became a main character in my own life
And stop wasting time on watching others'
wrongs so that I seem right
Drama producing more drama by feeding
negativity into my insight
I eat healthy I feel great my body and all connected
to me is whole and lacking no good thing
I only have songs of praises to my God to sing
For what He has done
How He blessed so His Chosen One
Hallelujah all Glory goes to our God
Turning an unlimited fold of what the devil robbed
I AM FREE
I AM GOD FOR GOD IS ME
WE ARE ONE
AND OUR PURPOSE ON LIFE HAS COME

THE WORLD KNOWS ME AS HIS CHOSEN ONE
I AM WHAT I SAY I AM
THEREFORE, WHAT I SPEAK WILL
MANIFEST WILL COME TRUE
THE LIFE YOU LIVE IS BY WHAT YOU
SPEAK AND THEREFORE DO
SO, SPEAK STRENGTH TO OVERCOME
WHATSOEVER IS WEAK!
YOU START IT AS YOU SPEAK THE NEXT LINE

I CHANGED MY SPEECH!

Love

My People receive this message from above
For what we need in this season is a flow of LOVE!
You know
Even the firefighters use water to put out
fire before it expands and grows
Water can be heated and chilled
Yet still
It doesn't explode it remains like calm water
Forgiveness is the answer my Sons and Daughters!
Forgive others that you might be forgiven yourself
Care for someone else
Other than just you
Your one act can initiate peace instead of
hate you are the breakthrough!
But sadly, for many money has a hold on you
You will be amazed
Of how many people die these days
Trying to get rich
Thinking that money will fill their emptiness
But they soon found
That it is not the money and what goes around comes around
Or maybe it is jealousy one of the weaknesses
of the flesh that all men fight
That is overpowering your life
The eyes are the gateway to the Soul
Watch what you behold
For all things that look good are not good for you
Stay true

No one is perfect we all make mistakes
This is part of the process as we grow in faith
Let us stop focusing on the problems and let us give thanks
Give thanks
For your strength
Not just physically but mentally and spiritually
Help others in need
You see when you plant a seed
When you help others succeed
You in return uplift you and everything that is connected to you
I dare not lie I told you before that you are the breakthrough!
Let us grow in diversity
Let us help our young men as they are
captured like slaves in our reality
Let us LOVE!
It doesn't cost a thing it is freely given from above
No more killing but more instilling
The Word of God
In this season, evil must relinquish
what was withheld or robbed
Speak those things that are not as though they were
Don't be moved by him or her
But move into your worth
Let your life make a positive difference on this Earth
Look beyond the daily and focus on the greatest need
Now cultivate your seed
For you were chosen for a reason
Trust if you are reading or listening to this now
that I AM is opening up your season
Of rebirth

Your new season of self-worth
Don't harden your heart
As I mention a new start
For this you have been waiting for
You want more
Then stretch your arms wide amongst the
sky and shout out to our Lord above
Shout out, now to open up the gates of Heaven and LOVE!
Trust, My Sons and Daughters
GOD SAID, "HERE IS MY LIVING WATER!"

LOVE

Satan's Master Plan

PASS THIS MESSAGE ON UNTIL
IT'S READ BY EVERY MAN

GENOCIDE
The systematic extermination or destruction
of an entire people or race
This was my main passionate challenge that I had to embrace

The extinction of man!
So, I concocted this death-taking master plan
I realized that if I could just corrupt the male
Manipulate him to believe that all-good dwells in hell
Yeah, if I could just seduce the head
Then their women and eventually their children will be misled!
I couldn't afford to make a mistake
Once I had their Souls, I needed them to stay in hell's gate
So, what shall I use as bait?

Having my hell soldiers die before or at least in their twenties
Hell yeah!
MONEY!
The route to all evils
A road deceived to bring richness and joy
yet, drives you straight to hell's land
Straight deeper to sin
Stealing Soul after Soul God will never win!

Now, how can I get man to feign for my treasures?

How can he believe that I'm his only and
last sense for pleasure in life?
How can I blind his sight?
Okay,
I have to steal his <u>education</u>
Where he has no other opportunity but to come my way
You know how the old saying goes
The best way to keep a slave is not to educate him
The less he knows the less opportunities he has
Making him easy to grab and control
Without knowledge he will have no thirst to attend college
He will seek me not God to make him whole
I will direct his hand
Selling drugs, guns, and sex will be
preached throughout this land
He will forever feel down and lack self-confidence to stand
He will abuse and misuse his queen
Keep her high, corrupt her soul, steal, cheat, and lie
Yeah, she will be my new drug fiend!
Bring her down!
Low self-esteem, dress half-naked, known for sleeping around
Yeah, she'll be my best prostitute in town!
He will destroy her worth!
By killing her dreams, my enemies in
which God granted her to birth
Yeah
Thank you man!
Because of you my name reigns throughout this land
You exactly have your women believing
that all men do is deceive

Because I used you
And you're too stubborn to learn God's
Words that's why you have no clue!

Now I have all I need
Through your hell born seeds
They kill just because you gave them the wrong look
And your young girls are hooked to lust!
Milkshakes and magical sticks
By the way, thank you entertainers for your negative words
You know your youth really do live out the words they heard
Now, all I do is just chill back and watch this mess unfold
My Master Plan is almost complete and whole
Yeah,
Man
This time I'm going to stand
Up and salute you
For you are the reason why hell on Earth is true
Oh, I know that you like to bet so let us make a deal
I dare you to run to God before your
life before your Soul I steal
Final fact
There's no coming back once you're mine
You'd better get right for you're running out of time

Yeah Man!
My Best Master Plan!

Devil

You will not win!

I accept the truth

That I was born in sin

That every day I fall weak but get right back up again

Confessing my sin to The Source

I command cancer will not steal my body or silence my voice

That childish thinking won't select my choice

In life changing decisions

That negative people's energy won't deter my visions

Hallelujah Anyhow

Devil,

I will praise the Lord even when I'm down and out

This battle won't last long I shout!

Yes,

I may sin

Yet

Devil you will not win

You're already defeated

No man formed against me shall prosper

Heed it

Devil!

Father

I lift my voice to you
Giving praise for all the marvelous things you do
When I was lost you led me home
When I sinned in your sight you still never left me alone
You called my name out of dust
Master in you I place my complete trust
Thank you, Lord,

Thank you, Lord, for shining your mercy on me
Thank you, Lord, for everyday I'm blessed to see
Tears of joy fall from my face
For your unfailing love I was chosen to embrace
I am your vessel where Your Spirit dwells
Use me Lord for with you I am destined not to fail
All shall hail Your Righteous Name
For as long as I live the Name of Jesus I will sing and claim!

Father
Let Your Kingdom Reign!

Your Time For Glory Has Come!

Hallelujah!

I heard the Lord call My Name

He said My Child now is your time to claim

Victory on this land

Come out of your pit and stand!

Birth what I have instilled within thee

Walk ever forward trusting in Me

Your enemies will be your steppingstones

In which the promise will grow

My words will be your source of knowledge

Which you must practice and know

I Am God

No man formed against you shall prosper

Stop putting your faith in him and her

Fall on your face humble yourself before Me

And My everlasting mercy

You shall embrace

Take one step at a time

The path to Glory, I will lead you to find

My precious Child, you are and forever will be a Child of Mine!

Visualize your dream

Recognize with Me as your King

That the sound of victory is not as far as it seems

Claim! Walk ever forward in Jesus' Name!

My Chosen One

Your Time For Glory Has Come!

I'll Still Be Blessed Every Day!

I say

Can I come through?

You see

Does my sassiness offend you?

The way I carry myself like a lady

Does my abundance of blessings drive you crazy?

Does my mentality

The way I transform my dreams into reality

Upset you

Do you envy how I always speak what's true?

Is it my confident walk?

How I command attention when people hear me talk

That scorns you

Or is it my anointing that brings me joy while

you're still feeling depressed and blue

Is it my beauty?

Both inner and out

That makes you scream and shout!

Or is it your own self-doubt?

You curse me with your eyes and disgraceful words

Yet, I took this moment to articulate so receive what is heard

I will rise

I will not feed into your childish lies

I will stand

I will conquer in Jesus' Name this Holy Land

I will succeed

I will believe

I will always be just me

Strong, intelligent, positive loving all my sisters and brothers

And yes, you too my enemy

Maybe if you got off your high horse

I would help you to make the right choice

Yet, you're too intimidated by my wisdom

and sweet-sounding voice

Have it your way!

I told you before

I'll Still Be Blessed Every Day!

Speak To Me Lord!

I UNDERSTAND WHAT YOU'RE GOING THROUGH
Yet now is not the time to give up on you
This internal battle between good and evil has reached its peak
I understand that during these seasonal tests
your mind, body, and Soul feels so weak
Yet, you must understand the consequences
of your past mistakes
You see,
So many of these problems you embrace
because you wouldn't obey Me!
I told you to drop that bad habit to leave that person alone
I told you to come back home but you stayed
Now you're frustrated because your dreams faded away
It is not your dream, but it is you who went astray
Yet, I understand
How difficult it is to prevail in this sinful land
This is why I granted you mercy this is why I heard your cry
Yet,
My Child my Words can't move while you're living a lie

So, Father God what am I to do?

I told you before that the answer lives in you!
You see,
You have to believe in order to retrieve
You have to give in order to win
You have to deny sin
You have to stay in my Word

You must receive what is heard

You have to give praise in order to rise

You have to pray in order for your sins to fade away

Notice

That I said You!

You are the only one to birth what is due

You should have known that I granted you freedom of choice

It's up to you to follow My signs and listen to your inner voice

Yet, no matter what

Don't you dare give up!

The race goes to those that finish what they have

started and continued to follow through

Clear you mind and erase all which hinders the better you

I understand, the question is do you?

Can you retrieve what is rightfully due to you?

Last and true, the answer is YOU!

Now Move and Know that I Am God!

I Won't Complain!

I Give Thanks
For everything that I have
For every trial that I embrace
I won't complain
But continue to give my Lord and Savior thanks!
I won't compare
What I have to others
When people succeed, I will uplift my sisters and brothers
You see,
I realize in order to receive more I must
appreciate what my Lord has given to me
To complain and to compare is to belittle God
for what He has done is not enough
That's why we're so easy to give our blessings up
Because it never was valued it wasn't truly
respected or held as our treasure
I will measure
My victory not by man but by my Lord
For only my FatherGodSpirit can grant me more
You see,
I expect nothing from man but to appreciate
everything that they are willing to give
You see, only from my God do I expect
to grant me the blessings to live
I Won't Complain
Only positive dream birthing words shall I speak
I won't define my life by where I'm weak

No weapon formed against should prosper
By Jesus Christ's stripes I am healed
I am made anew!
I Won't Complain and Neither Should You!

Have Your Way

Sovereign God of all Heaven, Earth, and Beneath
Forgive and have mercy on the ignorant words I so often speak
Only You
Know all the answers to why the righteous are forsaken
Only You
Created the foundations
Lord
King of Kings throughout each nation

Have Your Way
In my life everyday
It is only the Great I Am that I serve
That I aim to please
Receive my praises each day I fall down on my knees
No one can fulfill this endless hunger that I seek
No one can turn me from reaching Your Holy peak

How Excellent
How Marvelous
How Righteous
Is Your Holy Name
Only in You does my faith claim

Mold me as You see fit
Whatever is unclean wash away it
Purify my heart
Sight me on what I see

Have Your Way Jesus Christ!
Use me!

I thank You for Your Word
I praise You for my prayers were heard
I worship You the Holy Trinity
Have Your Way with me!
Until we meet on Judgment Day
Move by the words I say!
Father

Have Your Way!

I Will

Not crumble under pressure
I will accept my fate
I will rise over top of my mistakes
I will give what it takes to succeed
No matter Devil I will not give up on my dreams!

I didn't lose I gained strength
That's why right now at this moment
I can pray for my enemies and still give thanks!
For I will overcome
I believe that Jesus Christ died for me so that
I will have an opportunity to be someone
I will not fail
I refuse to give glory to hell
Devil, shake me, attack me, and stab me in the back
Hate me slap me
I may slip but not for long for I will remain on track
After I cry,
After I dawdle in Satan's deadly lies
After I question a million times why?
Why me?
I will reach down deep inside bringing
out all my unused energy
To leap over my fears
Devil, I told you before that I will make my way up these stairs
Don't you move
Don't you speak

For everything that you tried to kill!
Has been replaced with the words

I Will

Be Strong
For this test won't last long!

My Everything

My Most Sincere

I am who I am because in me you placed your merciful care

With you in my life I have no reason to ever fear

I am in love with you

My Most High and True

Never did you judge me for my flaws

Or perceive me to be less because of my mistakes

You always strengthened me to give what it takes to overcome

My Lord and Savior

You are my Chosen One

Jesus Christ

Your power overrules all mankind

You are that rare jewel that I have searched so endlessly to find

Let my words warm and soothe your heart

Let them penetrate straight to Your Soul

My Redeemer

I love you, for you first saw me whole

I may not have all the riches and gold

But, I do know that if I receive nothing just having you in life

Makes me feel complete and whole

You are my Father, my friend, my lover, my healer,

You are my Everything

In you my soul sings

Praises of joy

In you I find peace

Let us feast together at a table filled

with the Fruits of the Spirit

Filled with blessings that you desire to have

Let me grab
Ahold of your marvelous hand
As you so gently help me to stand
Let me speak of your unfailing love throughout this land
My Everything
You are all I need, and you I so faithfully believe
Forgive me for when I stray away from thee
Love me as you always do!
If I died right now know that you will always be my everything
That you will always be loved for just being You!

My Everything

Weakness of the Flesh

I'm so glad we met
Can I get in your head?
An evil king lying on his death bed
Thought
After I die who will be chosen as my head?
He pondered all through the night
Then daybreak he had his servant
summon his most loyal knights
The nine knights quickly arrived
For they knew that one of them would be
crowned king before the old man died
The evil king feebly said
One of you will be appointed my head
This decision is not easy to make
You see, evil can't afford any mistakes
For sure
The Good King is preparing for war
I will allow each one of you to plead your case
To why your evilness will lead this race
Before the evil king could choose who would speak
One of the knights in the back yelled it is I you seek!
He made his way to the front yelling I will lead this nation!
Yes, me Procrastination
I will make people delay
Let them doubt what they say
Help them waste everyday
Nothing will get done
Their dreams they will eventually give up on each one

It's me
I should be chosen to lead this evil army
Wait! Yelled another knight
It is I that will lead this evil army right
With a fatal kiss
Yes, me Laziness
They will not even move and grow satisfied with less
Like pigs they will lay and play in their mess
I'll make them tired
Can't even hold a job without getting hired!
You see,
I'll help them be their own worst enemy
It's I that should be called
To lead them all!

Please! Smartly said by another knight
It is I, Fear
That will control their lives
Let it be said
They will be too afraid to get ahead
Achieving their dreams
Their coward selves wouldn't even think of such a thing!
I will keep them in tears
Preying on their weaknesses and their most deadly fears
Whispering doubt in their ears,
The true evil king stands here!
Yes, me Fear!
Another knight confidently said I shall wear the crown!
As he made his way to the evil king's bed and knelt down
Your most faithful in which you always trust

Yes, me Lust

They will be too busy

Running around dizzy

Feigning for the next

All they will think about and live for is sex, sex, and more sex!

I'll make them war amongst themselves

Ready to kill when they share with someone else

Cuss, fuss, and mistrust

I'm the most deadly

Yes, me Lust

No!

Evil king!

No it's me

All should hail Jealousy

No unity

Will ever be found

I'll help them pull each other down

They will take, rob, and steal

If someone tries to move ahead, they will kill

Believe in what you every day see

It is I that should rule yes me

All hail Jealousy!

Move! Shouted an oversized knight

I don't have all night

I hold their deadly wish

Not them

Yes, I Selfishness

I'll make them live for themselves

Like me they won't care about anyone else

Team!

Don't make me laugh
They won't even care about helping each
other accomplish their dreams
Their model
I live to do me
Forget everybody
The Good King's army will be small
For their self-centered ways will help each other fall
I am the new king you wish
Yes, I Selfishness
A giant knight softly said
It is I evil king who has always led
Why should the truth be hidden?
I am your most favorite Hatred
While you're ill
For a fact I make nations kill
Each other
I make them disrespect their sisters and brothers
I stole the Good King's life before
And I'll kill Him down again if He steps up for more
For sure,
Evil king I created war!
So, why this bid?
When I should be crowned Hatred
A thin knight standing in front said
Can I pledge my defense?
I'm almighty Ignorance
I hinder them from knowledge of self
If people don't look or act like them,
they'll belittle everyone else

I help keep them down
Their true purpose for life will never be found
Please succeed!
Most of their stupid selves can hardly read
Or add
Their weaknesses are so easy to grab
Let it told, I will make them turn against
Why?
Because of me your new king Ignorance
Let me pass!
A knight yelled
Evil king they saved the best for last!
Trust this!
I will lead this army to victory yes me Stubbornness!
They will know right from wrong and
still won't change their minds
Their own stubbornness will leave them behind
To fail
Their own negative attitudes will lead them to hell
I'll make them believe that where they are
and what they have is the best
Not knowing every day that they're settling for less
There will never be oneness
Just as long as my name is Stubbornness
Can you hear the fat lady sing?
It's over I should be crowned king!
The evil king slowly rose from his bed
Saying I am ready to choose my head
Who was chosen?
Well, you have to be true

Which evil knight
Is ruling
YOU!
There it is!
The fat lady did sing!
This is who was chosen king!

Stay Honest With You!

I laid down my life so that you might be saved
I laid down my life. Question is, what have you gave?
Still sinning
Losing all along while you think you're winning
I laid down so that your Heaven on Earth might be found
I laid down while you run lustfully throughout your town
Still sinning
Losing all along while you think you're winning
I laid down my laws
So that you may claim what is rightfully yours
Yet, you read not
Do be aware that you're leading to a pitfall spot
Still sinning
Losing all along while you think you're winning
I laid down my life any moment yours too can come
Your sins will be judged just like everyone

So now you know
Question is
Where will your Soul go?

Here's a clue!
How are you living daily?
Stay Honest With You!

What Happened?

You used to call on My Name

Every day I would hear victory claimed

You used to read My Word

Tell me

When was the last time you heard?

My message

Do you tithe?

Don't you know without sowing seeds

your destiny will wither and die!

What happened to your promises you made?

What!

Gave up

Afraid to let go now you're stuck

What happened!

Wake up!

How are you using your talents?

The pieces that brings balance in your life

I plead surrender to Christ

Not to sin!

GOD is saying

My Child

What Happened?

I Am
All Woman!

I recognize my worth

For through the Blood of Christ Jesus

my Soul was granted rebirth

I Am

All Woman!

Making a positive difference on this Earth

I Am

All Woman!

Standing beside my man

Building a strong foundation in which my children will stand

I Am

All Woman!

Virtuous and called by Christ

To lead our people to eternal life

I Am

All Woman!

Not ashamed to say that sometimes I'm wrong

Yet, where I fall, I make it my mission to grow strong

I Am

All Woman!

Phenomenal, classy, and sexy indeed

I Am
All Woman!
For
I was born to succeed
Now Heed
I'm still Coming!

I Am
All Woman!

Midnight Soldiers

It's time to arise for the day
Armed shoot to kill chasing that devil away
Heed what I say!

This world is filled with hatred and deceit
With lies, deferred dreams that die,
And people clinging to that which keeps them weak
Souls dying daily in the streets
People pulling down others that they meet
Like you living in defeat
Shake the devil off
Before your Soul pays the cost
In Hell
Living every day to fail
Well, tell Satan no more and arise
The daybreak has come my Midnight Soldiers
Evil's wickedness must die
Yes, you
Stop living a lie!
Accept what I say as true
Do Right By You
I Cry!
Midnight Soldiers
Arise!

Virtuous Woman

Many sinners wonder where my secret lies

How I maintain my joy

While they cling to their cries

Why my blessing well never runs dry

And when I start to tell them

They think I'm telling lies

I say,

It's in the fiber of my bones

The Holy Spirit

Shining throughout my bronze tone

You see,

With Christ Jesus I'm never alone or have to fend for my own

I'm A Woman

Virtuously

A

Virtuous Woman

That's Me!

Poem inspired by Maya Angelou's poem Phenomenal Woman

A
Virtuous Woman

Is

Rare to find

A rock that survives the test of time

She appreciates her worth

A seed sowing on Earth

She raises her children to fear Christ

Living an abundant life

She is an excellent wife

She serves those in need

The Fruits of Spirit she stands on to succeed

A humble soul she possesses

Her sins she willingly confesses

She's above other women for she is not of this world

She lives to improve the future for all boys and girls

At her best she always seems

Her beauty is made reality of your dream

Her presence draws attention like flies to light

She is your golden pleasure at night

All seek yet few find!

A
Virtuous Woman
For She Is One of a Kind!

A Covenant Man

Apprehends his worth
This warrior takes responsibility for
birthing God's will on this Earth
His wife and children, after God come first
He doesn't allow Satan's pleasures such as
money and women to quench his thirst
He clearly understands what it takes to be a strong man
His calls are out of concern
It's his will to learn and please
Help ease
His wife's stress
He is for he recognizes that His Eve deserves the best
He walks in her anointing not intimidated by her success
Her placing God first doesn't make him feel less
He leads the family in prayer
His strength, courage, and wisdom he willingly shares
He communicates he sacrifices for goodness' sake
He comes to heal, build, and never take
He is a blessing sent from God a treasure rare to find
He is a leading man in his seasonal time
A Covenant Man
More of you are needed throughout this land
A Covenant Man
God Has His Hand On You
A Covenant Man Loves To Be True

My Covenant Man
I Love You!

Let This Be It

Let this covenant
Lord between You and me be meant
These words are sent
My Soul Says Yes
Let thy will be done
I accept as your Chosen One
Take my mind
Take my heart
Take my blood
Yet, give to me Your unfailing love
Make my enemies Your enemies
Fulfill my every need
And I will give you my life
My words are Your words Jesus my Christ
Yet,
Give me one taste
Give me just one touch
May there forever be just us
May all Glory go to Heaven!
May our Father God Spirit be endlessly praised
May all who choose raise
To higher Glory
Come out of your dry places!
Shake off the dirt, the worry, and the hurt
For I have come to claim My Own Name
As one
The end of the war has come
Stand up and listen

Pay closer attention

To what reads

I Am the water you seek yet you must believe that I am real

All thirst My Living Water shall kill

Feel My Spirit burning from within

Come to the Water my Child so that

Our true destiny may begin

You made a hit

No more let this be it

For it

Is here!

Don't be Afraid to Share!

Messiah,

I pray that what I write and that what I speak will come true
Savior,
I place all my faith in You

Your Holy Spirit lives in me
Guiding my footsteps and sighting all that I see
Everyday,
Father have Your way
In my life
Teach me to obey completing and living a fruitful life
To let Your Light shine all day and all night
My words are as humble as a child
My actions are made for the righteousness of You
Lord, allow this time to be my breakthrough
Remove all that which holds me back from eternity
Allow people to see You through me in reality
I pledge my Soul to You
My Forever Holy True
Master,
I want to die to myself
I want to eagerly grow to be someone else
Shine down Your Mercy on me allow Your
Forgiveness to enter into my life
Destroy all weapons formed against me with Your strong knife
As I write
As I pray
Christ, please have Your way!
Only you can do it

Only you can heal
Only you can feel
What lies deep within my heart
Messiah,
Let this day be our new start together
I pray that these words will dwell in You forever
Amen
I have faith that I will win
Victory is mine
I know that this is my time
Lord for this
Let My Light So Shine
Unto You

Messiah!

What I Speak Is True
My Lost Son This Is Just For You!

You can't serve two masters for one you will grow to hate
Receive this message and you will surely redirect your fate
You know
I sent my Angels numerous times to protect you from death
How easily you forgot how you overcame your constant threats
Yet, you still will not surrender all unto Me
You may not want to accept this but you're
still living out your own reality
Your own long-term fantasy
When I called you not for this purpose!
Let Me open your eyes to your deadly lies
You play
Everything you've planned has went astray
You will feel pain until you fall on your face
and worship my Sovereign Name
Until you claim
Me first you will forever thirst
For wholeness
Ask yourself,
How much time will you waste?
How many nights are you willing to paste?
Can't even sleep in peace
I gave you a purpose and you still allowed Satan to defeat
You surely know what I mean
I gave you a vision of what I dream to come true
Here on Earth
Start living in your true worth!

It's a shame

To watch you every day my Chosen One to

chase and stress over fortune and fame

Humble thyself

Come with an open heart to My House willing to receive Me

It is not people that you place your faith in no it's Me!

Pray to Me in Truth and in Spirit

Don't you ever worry that I won't hear it

I love you

More than I love myself

This is why I died for you

Now is, not tomorrow but now is the

time to labor for what is true

You must do right by you!

Come back home my lost son and I promise you

What you have been waiting for your breakthrough

It's not too late

You still have time to birth

What I've chosen you to birth

My Words must be heard on this Earth!

The last days are near

You must help my servant

To teach all to fear

Yes, You

What I Speak is True!

Amen

You have to die to yourself in order to win

Don't think! Let us just begin!

Remember, I Am the Beginning and the End!

I Come Before You

Moved not by degrees or wisdom but
by a will a desire by a need
Our future is depending on you to succeed
Raise up Body of Christ!
Raise up and share your gifts so that all may
have an opportunity to live right!
This is why you were granted life
To put others first
To break the cycle of the devil's deadly curse
No one knows all the answers
But together everyone can give what they have
Everyone can create a solution to whatever comes before us
We shall prevail just as long as in God we trust
Faith without works is dead
Our faith has led us to this destination
And with patience and determination all
of your dreams shall come true
The answers were already given to you
Listen to me as I speak!
We must sacrifice ourselves to make others
stronger where they're weak!
The war has reached its peak
The battle is already won
My Chosen One
Move
Move Move Move Move Move Move Move Move!
It's all true!

I Come for You!

Stand on My Word!
TRUST WHAT IS HEARD!

Recognize Your Worth!
I will lift up my eyes unto the hills, from whence
cometh my help. My help cometh from the Lord
which made Heaven and Earth (Psalm)

Grow to be whole!
For what shall it profit a man, if he shall gain the
whole world, and lose his own soul or what shall a
man give in exchange for his soul (Mark 8:36)

I Am your only reality!
Let not your hearts be troubled; ye believe in
God, believes also in me (John 14:1)

Eternity is true
In my Father's house are many mansions if it were not so, I would
not have told you. I go to prepare a place for you (John 14:2)

I died for you
Then said Jesus, Father, forgive them; for they
know not what they do (Luke 23:34)

I told you so
For where your treasure is there will your
heart be also (Matthew 6:21)

To kill sin
Lift up your heads, o ye gates, and be ye lift up, ye everlasting
doors, and the King of glory shall come in (Psalm 24:7)

To achieve more
Wait on the Lord, be of good courage and
he will strengthen thine heart
Wait, I say, on the Lord (Psalm 27:14)

To win

O taste and see that the Lord is good blessed is
the man that trust in him (Psalm 34:8)

This is how we should be this is what you need to see

Behold I stand, at the door and knock, if any
man hears my voice and open the door,
I will come into him and will sup with him,
and he with me (Revelation 3:20)

Heed what it says

A double-minded man is unstable in all his ways (James 1:8)

Stop living in fear

Let brotherly love continue. Be not forgetful to entertain strangers
for thereby some have entertained angels unaware (Hebrews 13:1-2)

I shall heal

Blessed are they which do hunger and thirst after
righteousness for they shall be filled (Matthew 5:6)

I know what you are going through

But I say unto you, love your enemies, bless them that curse
you, do good to them that hate you, and pray for them which
despitefully use you, and persecute you (Matthew 5:44)

This I gave

That if thou shall confess with thy mouth the Lord Jesus
and shall believe in thine heart that God hath raised him
from the dead, thou shall be saved (Romans 10:9)

Carry your load

A good name is rather to be chosen than great riches, and
loving favor rather than silver and gold (Proverbs 22:1)

Stop living for money, power, and fame

When I was a child, I spoke as a child, I understood as
a child, I thought as a child, but when I become a man,
I put away childish things (1 Corinthians 13:1)

Trust!

What shall we then say to these things? If God
be for us, who can be against us?
(Romans 8:31)

Let go of your grudge

Judge ye not, that ye be not judged (Matthew 7:1)

Here's a clue?

Ask and it shall be given you, seek and ye shall find, knock
and it shall be opened unto you (Matthew 7:7) If ye abide
in me and my words abide in you, ye shall ask what you
will, and it shall be done unto you (Matthew 7:7)

If you only knew

The harvest truly is plenteous, but the
laborers are few (Matthew 9:37)

Death will I kill

Who hath believed our report? And to whom is
the arm of the Lord revealed (Isaiah 53:1)

I need you to hear me as I speak

Be not deceived, God is not mocked for whatsoever a
man sow, that shall he also reap (Galatians 6:7)

My Child it's time to live a new way

And why call ye me Lord, Lord, and do not
the things which I say? (Luke 6:46)

It's time to move, use your head

But will thou know, O vain man, that faith
without works is dead (James 2:20)

Stand on my Word

This is your last reality

Jesus said unto him, I am the way, the truth, and the life.

No man cometh unto the Father, but by me (John 14:6)

TRUST WHAT IS HEARD!

Stand on God's Word!

Don't Bring Yesterday Into Today

Carrying that baggage throughout each day

Release

I say

Those old things, sure it's going to hurt

But now it's either it or you Child stay alert

Heed what I say

Don't bring yesterday into today

You know what,

Some people are just afraid of change

Just to confused, to used to being used

They wouldn't even know a good thing even if it hit them

Child get them!

Some people don't have their priorities in order

My dear son and dear daughter

It's about Souls!

It's about growing in wisdom until you're whole!

It's about you

Now is the time to complete what you are supposed to

But,

I never knew my worst enemy was me

O, how you block yourself from fulfilling destiny

But surely it shall come

Satan cannot block what I had declared

finished, surely it's done

The truth will come

When you learn and live what I say!

Don't Bring Yesterday Into Today

Father,

My source in which I was created to dwell
Father, help me ease this internal battle
between Heaven and hell
Once again
Father, I lay before your feet confessing my sins
I have corrupted, intoxicated my body with smoke
Cleanse my lungs before I choke
I have infested my body with sex
I have shared my temple with the next and the next
I have not honored my parents as you command
I have done forbidden deeds on this land
I have not taken care and appreciated
my blessings that you gave
Father, please forgive me so that I might be saved
Purify my heart
Circumcise that which is not clean
Father, I lean on your word
Father, I shout I pray these words are heard
What am I without You!
All that which is true
Father, I love you
I need you; I praise you; I worship you
Father, please direct me to what to do
I pray
Father, hear my supplications as I call on Your Name today!
Father, Show me Your way!
FATHER!

Give Me All

The Lord Speaks
Give Me all and I will deliver you from
that which keeps you weak
My Child
The road that you are traveling is dangerous and wild
I understand
The trials that you experience on this land
I know
How you yearn to grow
Yet,
You have failed to let go!

Let Me give you joy and peace
Let Me place in front of you an abundant feast
Receive these words
This truth must be heard
How are you spending your day?
Are you giving blessings to others so that
your blessings may be sent your way?

We have talked many times
Yet, your true destiny you have not labored to find
Obedience Is The Key!
That will unlock all the strength that dwells within thee!
You hear me,
Yet, you fail to understand the reason
My Child,
Now is your season

To retrieve

Yet, you continually fail for it is in you that you don't believe

Stop Running!

Stop Making Excuses!

Stop denying your inner voice

Stop making the wrong choice

Stop for death is true

Give Me all

So, I can strengthen you

Give Me all

My precious Child this is my final call

Give Me ALL!

All Power You Must Claim!

You come up with every excuse
Why you couldn't put your talents to use
You didn't respond when I called
I was trying to warn you before your fall
Yet, I stood at your door
I didn't even deny you when you didn't want
to dwell in My presence no more
I was there when no one else cared
I healed what Satan tried to kill
Yet, you left My Arm
Unprotected through the storm
I heard you cry
When life seemed so dark that you wanted to die
You are breaking My heart
How many times must we restart?
Come back home
Before you are left alone in this war
I will be there with opening arms for sure
My Child
It's time to live for more
All Power You Must Claim!
Say My Name!

Jesus!

I Will Pray For You!

I rebuke you devil for on my weaknesses you prey

I rebuke you devil for slowing me down everyday

I rebuke your negative words

I rebuke the gossip I heard

I rebuke your tricks

You see, you really think that you are slick

I rebuke my self-doubt

I rebuke the barriers that hinder me from living God's will out

I am anew I shout!

If I stay focused

And keep my eyes on the Lord

Moving one step at a time

My true purpose for life I shall find

So, devil

And the people you use

To keep me confused

Goodbye

I'm no longer getting high

Off sin

Did you hear me, or do I have to repeat it again?

You see

Today is the day

That I walk out on faith and live my Father's way

I rebuke

I rebuke

I rebuke

I'm going to say this everyday so better hit mute

Oh no,

There's no stopping until I reach the top
And the only thing that I will drop
Is you!
Devil you should have killed me then for now I have a clue!
Better yet devil

I WILL PRAY FOR YOU!

I Will Win Back Me Again

In the future I will become

But until then I must overcome

My daily flaws

Disciplining myself to follow my Creator's laws

I'm relinquishing that which keeps me weak

For if I continue to carry it I will surly embrace defeat

I have to take one day at a time

With perseverance victory I'm sure to find

No more contradicting myself

No more dying or sinning for someone else

I need a joy that no man can fulfill

A peace of mind knowing that my wounds will be healed

Father forgive me once again

Wash out the stains of my sin

Create in me a new heart

Lord allow me to experience a new start in life

Holy Spirit fill me with courage to live right

I can't look back

For just that quick glance will throw me off track

Don't remove my enemies

But grant me the strength to move above them

Lord with all that I am

I know that I will win!

Back Me Again!

Amen!

Every Day I Die!

Hear My Cry
Father, In the Name of Jesus!
I surrender myself to you I give you my trust!
No longer living for me yet surviving for us
I give you my dreams
Direct my life as you see fit
Lord, if it is in your will
Use me to heal
To be a human example of You!
Lord,
I surrender all because I know your Words are true!
Every day I die
Every day I die daily to my flesh
I live awaiting my season
Father, I know that there is a reason
Why I was granted life
To live right to pray for sight
To lay peacefully through the night
To be a soldier in the fight
Every day I die daily to my self-centered ways
To my disappointing days
I stop defending what others had to say about me
You see, I now live for victory
Every day I die
Just to be in the presence of the Lord
I cry!
EVERY DAY I DIE!

All Are Welcomed Yet, Few Are Chosen!

I STAND AT ALL DOORS!

The Choice Is Yours?

One day you are going to have to decide which side I claim

Hell or Heaven's Righteous Name

It's a shame

How many Souls die daily to sin?

It's a shame but our Savior died so that we might live again!

The question is?

How bad do you want Him in your life?

How bad are you willing to praise Jesus our Christ?

How bad do you want to save your Soul?

How bad do you want to be whole?

To be one with Christ

How bad do you want the Lord to restore your sight?

Then start tonight

Make some plans to move

Make the devil is already defeated your favorite tune

Trust, victory will be yours soon

Victory you shall claim

For you surrendered to Jesus' Sovereign Name

Rivers of living water pour from within

You said no to sin

The truth you're now beholding!

I told you before

All Are Welcomed Yet, Few Are Chosen!

How Much Can One Take?

If you're reading or listening to this know that it's not a mistake
You have to change your fate!

Have you noticed your attitude changing?
Have you noticed that your situation is becoming worse?
Have you noticed that nothing seems to quench your thirst?
Well, this is true
The Lord requires more from you!

He wants to take you farther than your everyday reality
He wants to make your dreams come true
Yet, I can hear Him say have you obeyed Me?

Everything that you have will crumble
if you don't heed what I say
I can hear the Lord shout stop wasting your granted day!
Make a way!
It starts in your home. Tell Me, what do you have to sell?
What do you possess that can take you
out of this hell experience?

Make no mistake
One day you will say Lord, "how much can one take?
I gave you all that is needed to succeed
Yet, you didn't have the faith to believe
You waited around
Now you're feeling down and confused
I told you what to use

But, you wouldn't listen as always you thought that
you had the power to change your own fate
Now once again you scream
How much can one take!
That's a question only for you to answer for
one day it will be too much to bear
How much my dear Child you say
When you finally get tired of living your
own selfish disobedient way
Make no mistakes!
Only you determine

How Much Can One Take!

These Dry Bones Will Live Again!

I'm calling all God's Seniors for this is your time to win!

Guess what's coming!

Healing, Self-confidence building, Dream

instilling, Self-doubt killing

In the Name of Love

The Lord of Heaven's Arm rose from above

He is moving on your behalf

For, the Lord rebukes the devourer for my sake!

And no weapon formed against me and my health shall prosper

The Word of God will change your fate!

Strengthening what is weak

The Lord Speaks,

Yes, there have been moments of silence

when I seem so far away

But, it was there My Child that I carried you all the way

Dream again!

Speak it into existence until you win

victory over sickness and sin

I have to let you walk on your own to build your faith in Me

Nothing is impossible with the Lord as your Almighty

Enjoy life

Get up and move in spite of the pain

In everything claim

Victory

I Hope you hear Me! My Chosen One!

What you prayed for has come!

Yet, without doubt you must believe
from the Beginning to the End!
That

These Dry Bones Will Live Again!

I Place My Hand On You

In the Name of Jesus
May you prosper in all you do
May you be led by the Holy Spirit too
May God use you
It's time, you have been called for such a time as this
Everything you had to endure brought you to this season
Know that there's a reason
Why we stand together!
Know that whatsoever comes God will shine His mercy forever
I want us to remember this moment
This first day
That God called us His way
To say
That the time has come!
I told you before that it's all about you my Chosen One!
Follow your inner voice
Allow My will to guide each choice
Move in the Great I Am Glory
Tell the world about His story
Save souls
Know that you were put here to make others whole
To sacrifice
To die for right
Look around at what I have blessed
This is your moment I confess
You did a job well done
To prepare you for this one
Take it not for granted

But just know that with each person God's seeds are planted

To grow

Let the whole world know

That Christ is the way to go

No one is perfect for we are all unique in our own way

All of you repeat what I say

I speak wisdom, courage, and strength

I speak that it's unto you Lord that I give thanks

Come in My temple and dwell within Me

I live to fulfill your destiny

Heaven here on Earth

Together we are about to walk into our worth!

Amen

So, let it be done

My Disciples

My Chosen Ones

The Process Has Begun

God's Power flow through!

As

I Place My Hand On You!

Loyalty

Is determined by a test
It's during that trying moment that the truth manifests
I confess
Are you for Me or against?
Pay close attention here's a hint

I watch you day after day
Use your time in such a childish way
Always on a quest to play
To lay
Down in sin
Asking yourself when will this end?
I watch you and how you speak
Using those words to make others weak
Claim defeat and self-doubt
I watch how you're so-called making your way out
I don't care who you are
From the ghettos to the highest paid superstar
You have needs that must be met
You have deadly secrets that you prefer to be kept
You are your own worst enemy
I know you hear me
For whom shall your Soul give glory?
To God or to a man-made story
The choice is yours to make
Just don't forget that with every test comes a change of fate
So debate
Before you do

Know that what man doesn't see the Lord is watching you
To determine what shall it be
Are you against or for Me?
Tell me!
Where does it lie
Your

Loyalty?

Can I Praise!

Can I just honor the one who raised!

My feeble legs

Who turned my world around!

Can I just get down!

On my knees

Saying thank you to the one who supplies all my needs

Hallelujah!

My Lord My Savior

Can I just open my Soul unto You?

Can it just reach You where we immerse as two?

Just me and you

Can I say thank you!

For all you have done and continue to do

Can I tell the world!

That dear Child dear woman dear man dear boy dear girl

No greater love is the love of God!

Is the love of Jesus Christ!

No greater love can transform your life

Go and glance into the sunlight

Go and become one with nature

Go and peace you shall find

Go for real this time

And read this Word sent to you

Go and experience your breakthrough

Yes, you

There are always going to be problems

There are always going to be trials

But child

You only have one life, so enjoy, appreciate
the new you, become one with nature
No, you don't need him or her
Just You
Remember it was God that raised your feeble legs!
Go and say

Can I Praise!

Give Me Glory

Jesus said, be a testimony of My life story
On the third day I rose
So that on this day I can uplift those that I chose
As My own
Today I make your temple My home
And you are not alone
Be patient as I have been patient with you
Grow in those areas that I purposed you to
For My own sake I look not on your sins or what you daily do
But dear Child
You have to want it for you!

Then Lord I speak,
I place aside what is weak
I changed by how I speak
So, I give You the highest glory
I live my life to tell your life's story
I may not have a church surrounding me right now
But In Jesus' Name Count Me In I'm Down

God said,
I gather My own that I have chosen for
even greater works I will do
Who ever thought that a Black President of
the United States could come true
Yes, right before your own eyes
And I tell you no lie

Something new something greater than you can
ever imagine is about to happen on this day
Make way
Here comes the Glory of the Lord
Fear not, for through this I make the rough places smooth
My Chosen Ones dance to a new tune
Soon, and very soon
All Will See
That the Great I AM has chosen this time to gather His Army
Do you remember the water gleaning with
sun rays coming straight towards you?
Do you remember what I spoke too?
I called you by name, you are mine
Now is, yes this marks the time
This is the day that I rose, on the third day
Write what I say
Straight for you
Continue My Story
Give Me Glory

I Give You My Glory!

A Bed of
Mistakes

My name I shall not reveal for this message is real
This is what it takes one wrong move to alter your fate
Drawing you deeper to sin, a soul breaking
maze that never ceases to end
This is where the story begins

I would like to consider myself as an intelligent sister
Practicing right from wrong
Working hard to keep my mind, body, and soul strong
Yet,
This weakness
It hunts, it preys upon my fate
An endless battle that I defined as
"A BED OF MISTAKES"

You See,
In the midst of me finding my Mr. Right I lost me
By corrupting my body
With each lay a piece of me was torn away
I found myself feeling less
Dating men that I knew couldn't give me the best
Their weaknesses became mine
Slowly Making It Harder To Find Myself!
Living for the dedication of someone else!

It hurts as I speak
For,
I strive to do right yet this bed keeps me weak!
It holds me back it pulls me in!
How can I stop this cycle of "Loving in Sin?"
What will it take!
To ease this pain from my
BED OF MISTAKES?

THE LORD SPEAKS
MY CHILD
You must fall back in love with you!
Stop contradicting yourself
Living in denial while blinded from the truth!
You must forgive yourself, let go, and move on
Surround yourself with positive energy
People who keep you strong!
You must pray for strength, courage, and wisdom
You must believe!
You must deny yourself in order to succeed!
You Must! You Must!
In This I Trust!
PRESERVE YOUR TEMPLE!
Seal It Tight!
Until I Grant You Your Mr. Right!
This Is What It Takes!

TO CEASE YOUR

BED OF MISTAKES!

Stop Doubting Yourself!

I don't know about you, but allow me to minister to myself
When I think of doubt I see an unstable person
And when I think of an unstable person
I see the Word "A doubleminded man is unstable in all his ways
You'd better pay attention to the Word on this page
For it's true
You say one thing and then the next you doubt you
In other words, you don't follow-through
I know, so now what do you do?
Shake off all that dirt
And work!
I don't care if you have to work from sunrise to sunset
Labor hard child to get your goals met
For this one life is short here today then gone the next
Stop worrying about everyone else and keep yourself in check
Oh, I'm thanking God that we met
For what is to come unto you
Child if you would just labor for the right
thing what a blessing that awaits you!
Doing what you were truly called to
Well, I think that's enough of beating up on you
For even after I speak I bet you still continue to do you!
What is it going to take?
To make
You see
That greater is the God in me
He shall have His way
Even if you have to pay

For your disobedience
You're no better than someone else!
If you want to live then

Stop Doubting Yourself!

Slippery Slide

I'm going to take you to the hell side

Where Satan lies

So let it be told

This goes out to all my sinners, pay close

attention for this you must behold

Dear One,

I grabbed you through your father and mother

yeah that's where I grabbed them

You see, your whole family was infused in sin

You too know where our bond begins

I was your fear kept dear to your heart

I knew I had you near right from the start

And you believed me too!

I kept you so busy that you could never focus on you

Trust wherever you are in life

You could have been ten times higher than that height

I killed you with my tempting knife

Yeah right,

Remember when you tried to improve when you tried to let go

Now, you should know

That I don't release easily

Once I got you there's no leaving me

Without a cost

You never wanted to admit that I was your boss!

Lust, Greed, Pride, Stubbornness, and Hatred had you lost

I claimed you for the dead

When you became too afraid to move ahead

When you grew comfortable in your spot

When you gave up the Word drop
Yet, every day the Lord knocked
At your door
Pledging with you to live for more
And you ignored Him too
That's when I finally realized that I had you!
I bet you're reading this right now
Wondering how did I get so far down
Into sin
I bet you're saying now I'm ready to win!
But Daughter and Son,
You can try but I'm always going to use someone
To bring you back
You can't leave me without a fight now that's a proven fact!
You can run but I'll be back
To knock you off track
You can run but you can't hide
It's so easy to slip on my side
What I say, Slippery Slide
You can run but you can't hide
I won't rest until you die!
See you on the hell side

Slippery Slide!

You Can't Love Two Masters!

Lord,

Redeemer of lost Souls born to win

Forgive me and have mercy on my sin

Lord,

My will is strong yet, my flesh is weak

In the midst of my sin I still seek after you

You see,

I know that it's only through You will I win

Redeemer let the process begin

As I visualize

I fantasize on the person that I could be

Intelligent, beautiful, and not afraid to express my spirituality

But, this other side I know as me holds me back

Keeps my priorities off track

The true war

Is not amongst this world

No, it's in you!

So many Souls are lost because they didn't make it through

What about you?

Are you hearing the inner voices?

Guiding you and your life choices

Or do you turn your face

Not putting forth any effort

To change your fate, before hell you embrace

Just think

No good days

Lay ahead in hell

Every achievement you had fell

Nailed to a bottomless pit
Sleeping, bathing, and eating in your
own mess I hope you hear this!
Hollers for help you visualize and fantasize about the other side
Known as Heaven on Earth
Where there's joy, peace, and freedom from this curse
Never again will you thirst
It's already done
Yet, you must sacrifice yourself Chosen One!
You must die to your flesh
Killing everything that is not in Me!
Only then Child will I show you mercy
You can't ignore and call Me Lord!
Yes, this is for him and her!

YOU CAN'T LOVE TWO MASTERS!

Chapter 3
GOD'S LOVE

*"For God so loved the world, that he gave his only begotten
Son, that whosoever believeth in him should not perish,
but have everlasting life." (John 3:16 KJV)*

*"Dear friends, let us love one another, for love comes from God. Everyone
who loves has been born of God and knows God. Whoever does not
love does not know God, because God is love." (1 John 4: 7-8 NIV)*

*"Though the mountains be shaken, and the hills be removed, yet my
unfailing love for you will not be shaken nor my covenant of peace be
removed," says the Lord, who has compassion on you." (Isaiah 54:10 NIV)*

*"No, in all these things we are more than conquerors through him who
loved us. For I am convinced that neither death nor life, neither angels
nor demons, {a} neither the present nor the future, nor any powers, neither
height nor depth, nor anything else in all creation, will be able to separate
us from the love of God that is in Christ Jesus our Lord." (Romans 8:37-39)*

God's Love

Dear Adam

Dear tasty sweet

Each day I pray for the day we meet

No more drama no more pain

It's my honor to claim

Your last name

I proclaim

I can't wait to wake up in your arms

I can't wait to keep you and our family strong

I proclaim

Our love will last forever long

Dear Adam

Dear Friend

Our souls shall immerse until the end

We were created to win

Your soothing words are constantly heard

Your tender care is willingly shared

Your inspiration allows me to survive within this nation

You are all I need

You are the rock in which I succeed

You are my blessing sent from above

An Angel brought forth to show me an example of

GOD'S LOVE

Mr. Brown

I watch you from afar
You are my shining knight
My Superstar
Tall, dark, and handsome with a touch soft as baby's skin
Good loving that you despise to end
Yet,
I must be true
MR. BROWN
I Love You!

I love your dominant way, the positive words you say to me
With you I long to be
I love the way you work the patience that you possess
I love your firm body and lying on your broad chest
I must confess
MR. BROWN
You are the best!

I love you for who you are and for the future that shall come
Bride and Groom
Where God is held as number one
I didn't think that I could be tamed
For,
Men have played so many games with me
To be loved was becoming just a fantasy
MR. BROWN
Tell me how you feel does forever seem real?

Can you love me the way that I was blessed to be loved?

There's no me without loving our Father from above!

For,

I am your gift and a gift you are to me too

My love

My other half

I want to remain true

I want to be the woman

You hold at night

I want to be the woman

Who takes care of you when you're not feeling right!

I want to be the woman who mothers your kids

I want to be the woman who constantly gives

To make our foundation strong

To make our relationship last forever long

I want to be the woman who says I do

I want to be the woman

Who loves you when you're old or feeling blue

MR. BROWN

The question is

Do you want the same too?

If the answer is

Yes

Then you and only you must provide our nest!

You are the man and a man I shall allow you to be

The head of our family

I will submit only when you submit to our Lord!

For,

If you're leading, I want to make sure that God is leading you

MR. BROWN I LOVE YOU!

Our future shall grow

Yet,

We must learn and practice to put each other first

We must not allow any other man to quench our thirst!

We must motivate and push each other

We must compromise for the good of one another

We must move for our future shall flourish

The love of each other we must nourish

What else can I say?

But we have found our balance that will help us live each day

MR. and MRS. BROWN!

TRUE LOVE IS FINALLY FOUND!

My
Rose

I Chose
To speak with you today
About that childish way
You live
Pay close attention I come to give

You know what, you've been through much
Most of the time by yourself there really wasn't an us
That lack of guidance forced you to survive on your own
It's hard to raise a house when you were never raised in a home
And I know you feel alone
So, you search you seek
Men that participate in where you are weak
You struggle for self-identity, purpose, and affection
You struggle for the need of protection, of want
So, you hunt
That which is no good
Dating brothers in the hood
That lack wisdom and insight
Stop dreaming of being somebody's wife
And start building yourself!
Stop living by the past opinions of someone else!
And start healing
No more tears
No more being controlled by your deadly thoughts and fears
Even if no one cares

You still will labor

Even if you're robbed, you still will love all your neighbors

For, it's your time to blossom

My Rose

I Chose

This just for you

Test Me and watch your breakthrough!

God knows!

That this chapter in your life has been closed

He said, that this is the day

I CHOSE!

My

Rose

Sister to Sister

Can I Speak to You?
You see, I understand what you're going through
Yet, the Lord told you to believe!
To allow His Grace to fulfill your needs!
Love your enemies for they make you strong
They toughen your skin, and they teach
you how to control your emotions
So, go right along
With the change
I know this period this transformation may seem strange
But, the better you will come!
How can you touch millions without
experiencing pain Ms. Chosen One!
Breathe!
Call on the Name of Jesus to maintain your
joy and push forward on to succeed!
You are not alone in this war
For sure, many are fighting battles daily as you
Yet, you must accept what is true
You must believe
Millions are waiting on you to lead
Did you just hear what was said?
You are not the tail yet the head!
Move in His Glory! The world is waiting to hear your story!
Keep it coming they're hating on your success
Keep it coming always give your best through any twister!
I'm speaking from the heart
SISTER TO SISTER

Healing Men and Women

You've been through hell yet, survived each test
Now you are entering into a season of rest
Here you must pray, fast, and confess your sinful deeds
In this season of loneliness, you must lean
on God to provide your every need
This is one of your greatest seasons in life on Earth
Through a series of transformations, you
will come into your true worth!
Unbearable pain will you experience from letting go
All the worldly treasures and pleasures
that you've come to know
Realize that changing from the inside
requires discipline and patience
And unshakeable faith!
The key to victory is to remain joyful in the midst of the storm
Always praise and give thanks!
Be of good courage My Healing Child the Lord speaks!
You have already been victorious over the
devil; no longer can he keep you weak!
Uncertainty and a feeling of being
overwhelmed you will embrace
Yet, just remember the prize goes to the
runner who finishes the race
Repent with deep sorrow and overflowing tears
Lay down on Me all your doubts, troubles, and fears
Healing Men and Women
Heal by Yourself!

This season is your dedication to Me
not the world or someone else!
Stop your disbelief
You already know trust only in Me!
This you will find
Pain may endure through the night, yet
joy comes in the day time!
Everything that you dream for
With obedience to Me I will bless you with more
Surrender all
And diligently follow the light
Healing Men and Women
Right now is your season to reform your life!
Yes,
It's time to choose right!
BE STILL!

Healing Men and Women
Heal!

Is Your Will For True?

Turn Your Wicked Ways Before Death Gets The Best Of You!

I WILL PASS THIS TEST!
I will remain strong fighting through the storm
Until my soul is put to rest!

YOU CAN TAKE MY CAR!
You can deceive my mind that I was left
behind while others go so far!
Yet, like my ancestors I steal away to freedom,
to Jesus, who is my guiding star!

YOU CAN TRY TO TAKE MY HEALTH!
Yet, God is a jealous God and will not
allow anything or anyone to harm
What He is using Himself!

YOU CAN TAKE MY HOME!
Yet, I will always be sheltered in the Arms of God
Who said that He would never leave His Child alone!

YOU CAN TRY TO STEAL MY JOY!
Maybe when I thought as a child, now
I live as an adult in the Word
Who no longer cries over broken toys!

IT'S IN THE WORD!
My Soul just gets happy for I now understand
the knowledge that I heard!

I MAY LOOK A MESS!

Clothes might be old, yet I walk proud amongst any crowd
Until it's my time to be blessed!
I confess!
It is my Lord who told me My Child you are the best!
For, if I live for man I live for less!

YOU HAD ME BELIEVE!

That I was only meant to follow and not to lead
That I had to possess these material things in order to succeed!

WELL, YOU'RE WRONG!

I will pass this test standing firm or moving strong!

YOU SEE!

Satan's pleasures are quick
It's like a fiend searching for his or her next fix!
While my Lord's blessings are forever long
They don't kill in time, yet they heal
and build to keep you strong!

I WILL!

For, I know where I stand!

I WILL

For, the devil is already defeated
and God's breath is the breath of life on this land!

I WILL

How About You?

IS YOUR WILL FOR SATAN'S ARMY
OR IS YOUR WILL FOR TRUE?
I Pray
Starting Today

TURN YOUR WICKED WAYS BEFORE
DEATH GETS THE BEST OF YOU!

PROVERBS 8:36
But he that sinneth against Me wrongeth his own soul:
All they that hate Me love death!

It's Been a Long Time Coming

But, I made up in my mind
That I'm fighting back for my life this time
You see,
This battle is not mine, but the Almighty's
I plead the Blood of Jesus over these words which are True!
Scripture says, "If ye have faith as a grain of mustard seed, ye
shall say unto this mountain, remove hence to yonder place;
and it shall remove; and nothing shall be impossible unto you!"
I will speak
Only strength even if I'm weak
I will confess
That by the Blood of Jesus my health finds rest
My breathing is at its best
There is no cancer and disease found
amongst my body and chest
These dry bones are renewed by my faith
Without doubt I give my God His highest thanks!
My tongue is filled with the power of life and death
I now kill in the Name of Jesus any threat
Brought to me!
I am just now beginning my true destiny!
Praises I will sing unto the world for what the Lord has done
How He healed my body and rebuked the
devourer for my sake each and every one
No weapon that is formed against my health
will prosper unless it's my Father's Will
Even then my God doesn't give me
More than I can bear

I now cast all my worries, cares, pains, and fears
Unto my Lord Jesus Christ
It's Been a Long Time Coming!
But I'm Fighting for My Life
Body Be Thee Made Whole
It's Been a Long Time Coming
Yet, God Is Not Ready for My Soul!
I Speak It Therefore This I Know!
It's Been a Long Time Coming
But, I'm Not Ready to Go!

It's Time To Get Saved!

Lord I pray
That I may bury my past and live a new way
You see,
I don't know about you, but this goes out to me

I'm tired of living in sin
I'm tired of trying when everything I do comes to an end
I'm tired of being unhappy no matter how much I try to smile
I'm tired of smoking, sexing, and acting wild
I'm tired of living in filth
I'm tired of being motivated by guilt
I'm tired of feeling incomplete
I'm tired of honoring the word defeat
I'm tired of feeling less
I'm tired of thinking that I don't deserve the best
I'm tired of not believing in me
I'm tired of procrastinating in not making my dreams a reality
I'm tired of hurt
I'm tired of being hit by dirt
I'm tired of ungodly women and men
I'm tired of my body being used for the victory of sin
I'm tired! I'm tired!
Lord, I must confess
I'm tired of feeling useless!
I need direction, I need protection, I need unconditional love!
The Lord Speaks My Child
You must be washed and covered under My Blood!
You must move, you must believe, you must open My door

Thereafter you will no longer be tired any more!
If you feel as I do
Your greater purpose wants to come through
Open, unchain, and release
DON'T BE AFRAID!
I'm talking to you My Child

IT'S TIME TO GET SAVED!

I
Knew!

I KNOW

What I was supposed to do

But,

My people came through!

I KNOW

That my bill was due

But,

I'll act like I had no clue!

I KNOW

That my money could have been used more efficiently

But,

That outfit or thing caught my attention!

I KNOW

How a lady is supposed to act

But,

If they didn't see me, it's not a fact!

I KNOW!

I KNOW!

I have work to do

But,

I'll do it tomorrow and row with you!

I KNOW

Girl Grow!

I KNOW

Then let it show!

I KNOW

You must!

I KNOW

Believe and Trust!

I KNOW

What are you waiting for?

I KNOW

Close the

Casket Door!

I

KNEW!

Thank God That I Was Saved

I mean God himself snatched me from the power of the grave!

And I made it through

Heaven is now my home too!

Because I believed

That no matter what Jesus would lead

Me home

No more feeling lost and alone

And It's true

God prepares himself a mansion just for you!

And who would have known

That this day would come so quick

Like we face the taste of that last hit

My last word is to quit!

Put down that which kills

And let the Word of God instill

A peace that surpasses all man's

understanding here on this Earth

Quit feeling sorry for yourself and labor in your true worth!

You are greater than you think

Don't sink

But swim

Forget her or him

And love you!

That one Word is your breakthrough!

What more can I say

But that I will miss you each day

So, don't mourn too long for I grow more

blessed and blessed I'm "A-Okay"

And may this bring a blessing your way
For I claim
That time gets the best of us, so don't feel
or live in guilt, sorrow, or shame
For I of all people truly understand
How the pressures of this life can weigh down on a man!
Making it feel impossible to stand
But, God is greater
I speak from this day forward God is moving it all in your favor
Thank God for being able to witness
To tell all right now to use this as evidence
That Heaven is real!
And that Jesus Christ our living sacrifice
Paid the ultimate price
For our salvation!
Let us live differently than this nation
Let us grow in forgiveness, understanding, and patience
Let us LOVE!
Love as our Heavenly Father Commanded from Above
For this journey, this transition, we all must embrace
I promise you will not leave the same as
you first entered into this place
For while I was speaking the Holy Spirit
cleansed with Jesus's Blood
I'm telling you from this day forward you just
received another dose of God's Love
For my death
Was meant to help you all overcome any threat
My death brought life
And thank you all for keeping me in Christ

For as I saw the darkness then I saw a bright light
And I SMILED like I have never SMILED before
My Last Words Are Thank You Lord!
For only through Jesus Christ is there more!
With all that I AM when God himself breathed life through
Feel this my loved ones for I forever love you!
Amen
Welcome GOD In!

(In Honor Of Our Beloved Your Words Now Live Forever!)

I'm A Soldier for The Lord

While I'm Here

I will save souls growing in wisdom until I'm whole

Let me share!

I'm A Soldier for The Lord

On the battlefield!

I learned that only with Jesus do I receive more

Do the real me, come through

While I'm Here

I'm going to love both me and you

Even when I'm wronged

I'm going to place my faith in my Savior's Strong Arm

You see it's so true

That fighting

For Heaven's Armies brings forth your breakthrough

I'm going to praise

I'm going to allow the Holy Spirit to raise my feeble legs

To empower my mind

I'm going to allow The Great I Am to direct my time

Here on Earth!

I speak it

In the Name of Jesus, I live and flourish in my true worth!

I Am A Soldier!

Daily I fight sin

Satan's deadly weapons, but this Child of God was born to win!

Victory is mine

I speak it in faith that this is my time

To stand before a nation and let my light shine

All glory be unto my Lord and Savior

For, it was His self-sacrifice that brought me favor
So let the next battle begin
I promise you at the end
I will stand!
God's Glory will be known throughout this land!
I will receive my long waited for crown
As my soul rises to my Father's throne
I will hear like thunder in the sky welcome home
Well done My Chosen One
What you imagined; I grant you more!
Because you faithfully labored and declared that
I'M A SOLDIER FOR THE LORD!

Keep
On!

I'm Going
To Keep On Keeping On!
Fighting my way through the storm
In the Holy Name of Jesus Christ
I'm going to fight sin with the Word of God
Until I receive eternal life
I'm going to speak
Those things that are not as though they were
For Scripture said,
That I am not the tail but the head
That I am more than a conqueror through Jesus Christ
I'm going to love all my enemies
Even if they were wrong and I was right!
I'm going to move mountains
Things that once held me back
I'm going to encounter
That enemy in me that once kept me off track
I'm going to shout!
Praising the Lord in advance for my way out!
I'm going to dance in the Spirit
I'm going to continue to pray until my Father receives it
I'm going to move
Shaking off all the dirt while I sing to a new tune
I'm going to work
Laboring in spite of the hurt
I'm going to give!

Even when death is near

I'm going to claim in my Savior's Sovereign Name live!

I'm going to fall on my knees humbling myself

I'm going to lift up someone else

Until the day I die, I'm going to forgive those

that persecute me, back stab, and lie

For Scripture said forgive others that we may be forgiven

I'm going to keep on keeping on and living

Giving you this opportunity to declare

Your inherited Kingdom rights

I'm going to speak wise insight from night to dawn

Child of God

KEEP ON

KEEPING ON!

My Wife

My other half
One of my greatest gifts in life
I pray that these words are true
For God blessed me when He blessed me with you
You are my breakthrough
The mother of my seeds
The reason why I believe
That all things are possible for with you I succeed
You are all I need!
Beautiful as the day that we first met each other
My faithful friend and my treasured lover
I discover
A different piece of joy of love in you each day
I appreciate the encouraging words you say
And how you sacrifice to help bring balance my way
This is true
In my eyes there is no other woman greater than you
My precious flower
Worthy of each second, each minute, and each hour
That we share together
I pray may our love last forever
May you know
That this is your season to prosper to grow
To let your granted gifts show
I care for you
Every day that I'm blessed to see with you
Is like a dream come true
I don't just love, but I'm in love with you

If I had the world

I would give you the moon and the stars

For my feelings for you reach that far

Beautiful you are

Until death

Your treasures of my heart will be kept

For life

For no one can fill what I feel for you

MY WIFE

MY EQUAL JUST YOU AND ME
A LOVE THAT WILL LAST FOR ETERNITY

My Husband

MY LIFE

I just had to pause for a moment to tell you

that it's truly an honor to be claimed as your wife

You're one of the choices that I made unshakably right

Each night

I pray

That God would grant me another day

To be surrounded by your unfailing love

To be cared for as our Lord commanded from above

How can I truly say?

That throughout this time

My feelings for you grow more day by day

Each moment we share brings something brand new

You see,

What many hope for, my husband, you are my breakthrough!

No one said that love was easy, everyone experiences pain

But I swear

Throughout each of our trials we never lost but we gained

It's a strange

Feeling that I feel

Please receive what I speak as real

I never knew pure love until pure love came my way

I never knew the true meaning of unconditional

Until I said yes that day

Yes, to being set free

Yes, to having a life partner that stands beside me
One of these days my soul on this Earth shall be no more
One of these days I shall be in the home of the Lord
So, I'm going to speak these words which are true
I learned to appreciate life when I met you
You gave me meaning and purpose to stand
You supported my dreams to take dominion on this land
I will shout to the world that I have a phenomenal man!
No maybes or ifs
My shining knight, you are my greatest gift
By faith I speak even after death our souls shall embrace again
For we were born to win

MY HUSBAND

My Godly Man!

The God in him
Which helps me stand
May our love now be known amongst this land
For it's true
Your unconditional love has kept me sound
as I undergo my breakthrough
As I become myself
You have accepted me before I was known to everyone else
My funny ways, my trying days
You still remained
Believing that my heart one day you would claim
As your own
My Godly Man
It's time to come before God so that we will
continue to have a blessed home
As you stand
As the power of God overtakes you
My Godly Man
By your side I shall be
Praying that our Creator shows His mercy unto you and me
At last you are mine
At last love has found itself in time
Clinging to us
My Godly Man do trust
That wherever life shall take us to
My Godly Man
The God in you I will hold its memory forever through
You are not just my lover, my protector

My affection shown by Heaven on Earth
But you are my best friend
I hope that whatsoever God has for you shall it begin
By the Blood of Jesus Son of God, I speak win!
So let it be known amongst this land
If God is for you than who can be against you
My Godly Man
Stand!
For God has shown favor to you

My Godly Man

IN THE BEGINNING

My Eve

MY RIB
Breathes life through you
I thank God that my need has come true
The day God created me to bring life to you

Each moment we share I fall deeper in love
I experience a piece of Heaven in your arms my love
My personal angel sent from above

You are my life
A queen that I am honored to call my wife
Let me anoint you with the finest oils rejuvenating your skin
Let us embrace as one when you let me in
The softest place on Earth
Every day I live is to recognize and appreciate your worth!

Oneness we will share
One heartbeat one soul I am who I am my rib
For with you I am made whole
With you joy fills my soul
I promise until death do us part
My love will remain the same as our first start
Amen
Let Love Win

I Believe!
In You
MY EVE!

Where I'm From

Studying the Black man from which I came
and yearn to live my life with
Has placed my soul in a constant fit
You see, where I'm from
So many of my brothers are struggling to become someone
Not knowing that the answer lies within
My brothers you must learn and practice
the deterioration of sin
The devil attacks the head
While sisters are misled
Nothing on this Earth is free
You must plant the seeds to instill your family's tree
Look at your presence, it conceals the true essence of you
Now let's keep it gangster, let's keep it true
You disrespect your sisters because you
have no respect for yourself
Learn to unconditionally love someone else
You work for the man
Of course a job you can't stand
A job with no growth
Chained by the collar until you choke
Entrepreneurs
Your establishment is yours to run
Use your talents, not a gun
When testing the manhood of who's number one
Have you ever heard that quality is better than quantity?
My brothers you must wake up and see
That the only person who holds you back is you

Strength and courage it takes
We all make mistakes
I plead
Give your life to Jesus Christ and you shall succeed!
You must first come through Him if not, why get married?
Allow both of your souls to be buried
In hell for this way you did choose
This is why so many relationships lose
Their worth
Man and woman were not to love like this on Earth
Do right
Provide a home then make her your wife
Treasure your kids and you shall receive eternal life
In Heaven

Gentlemen Thug

GENTLE YET ROUGH
A deadly high like a fiend you just can't get enough
FIRM YET SWEET
Just a thought makes your flesh weak
With those master techniques between the sheets
Heats your spine
A Gentlemen Thug is one of a kind
Is that husband material a woman prays to find
A father to his kids and a supplier to his wife
His sole purpose for living is to lead his family right
Intelligent as they come
Yet, he is not the one to mess with
A Gentlemen Thug will destroy if hit
A shining knight
Filled with chivalry and always polite
Good loving all day and night
Faithful too
When he commits there's no other woman but you
He wears the mask
Just when you thought you knew him, he'll switch up on you
He is first class, saving the best for last
I'll tell the truth I'm addicted to this drug
You see, nobody can satisfy me like my **Gentlemen Thug**

Because I Love You So Deep My Brothers, I Have to Speak!

You were made in His image therefore; God is a part of you
The question is, my brothers, are you
walking in His footsteps? Stay true
This poem is dedicated to you!

DO RIGHT BY YOUR WOMAN
For this blessing was granted upon request
She is your treasure chest where your most
important jewels nest to grow
Never be afraid to let your love show
She is the rock in which you stand
The overseer while you're out hunting the land
She is your comfort, your peace of mind
Worthy of your dedicated time
She brings life to your world
Blessing you with a little boy or girl
Yet, you must remain faithful for temptation will come
Stealing your bond of your beloved one
Without trust
There's no us
Without honesty
There can never be a free conversation
Speaking the truth without hesitation
To top that, here's another fact
Cheating becomes easier to do

Caught up in so many women that you lose respect for you!

Then it festers down

A misdirected mindset is found

You see, if you don't respect yourself

Then how are you going to respect someone else

You say, forget her, another woman will come my way

But your soulmate only comes once did you pass her by?

Loving others while living a lie

Take back that which was stolen

Start unfolding our present-day struggles that poison our men

My fathers, it's time to stand to band against sin

The Devil is already defeated therefore; he can never win!

Don't just birth but raise your child

There are too many fatherless children running wild

What! Didn't you know that your presence illuminates the room

Make her an honest woman, your bride and you her groom

Get in tune with her ways

Acknowledge what she says

Do for her not only on special ceremonies

but each and every day

Let her know that she is truly a blessing

that God has sent your way

You are the head for God did say

Bring forth man with a breath of life calling this a good day

Yes, I'm talking to you my son for you are the chosen one

Join the Fight!

DO RIGHT BY YOUR WOMAN!

When Will I Know
If I
Found Mr. Right?

He nurtures your soul
Where you are unfilled, he is whole
He supports your dreams
Willing to work together as a team
Without a doubt, trust is there
Your weaknesses and strengths
You are both willing to share
Willing,
What a word
That best describes the characteristics of your
soulmate
It's his will not to take!
Yet to add, to build, and to grow
When you find Mr. Right
There's no question you just know
Better yet, it will plainly show
Your house is in peace
Your pressures are released
The Fruits of the Spirit
dwell
Your mind, body, and soul are well
With him, you will never fail!
He accepts you for who you are
His own personal superstar
He understands your need to succeed in life

Your backbone for support
Your defense, your shining knight
Your golden pleasure at night
There are no secrets to hide
Standing together side by side
Till, Death Do You Part
Only He
Will Hold the Treasures
To Your
Heart!

Through
The Grace Of God
I Understand

NOW IS THE TIME TO HELP MYSELF STAND!
To Be
God's Leading Lady

TO BRING MY TALENTS OUT!
To birth
My dreams without fear and self-doubt!

I AM
All that needs to be

I AM
Because I unconditionally love me!

You See,
I AM
Somebody!

TO YOU THAT READS!
You must believe!
Don't give in!
You are destined to win in life!
A process filled with trials and strife!

I PLEAD!

When you feel weak

Everything will tell you no

Yet,

It's GOD that you must seek!

TAKE TIME TO YOURSELF!

Become one with nature

MEDITATE!

Open your eyes and realize that only you determine your fate!

MY CHILD

YOU ARE NOT A MISTAKE!

FINAL RHYME

It Doesn't Happen Over Night, Live One Day At A Time

THE TRUTH GOD'S GRACE
YOU
SHALL FIND!

Strong Woman!

Still coming in spite of the pain
Daily breaking down barriers to gain
Stability in life
To live Christ-like
You Go
Strong Woman!
I must pause for this moment cause
For a deeper touch
You see,
I know Strong Woman that sometimes the road
Gets rough!
There's no one to count on but you
Have to help others while you too
Are trying to make it through the storm
Hold on Strong Woman
This test, this mess, won't last long!
Our Father,
Feels your pain
It gives me great pleasure to announce that from
This day forward victory you shall claim!
For the devil is defeated
Strong Woman
Now is your time, heed it!
Go ahead and claim
Whatsoever you want and desire in Jesus' Name
If only you believe
If only you receive what you said
Only then will it come to pass

Strong Woman

I dare you to speak first class, good health, balance, and gain

Still keep coming, in spite of the pain

Strong Woman

This Is Your New Day

Have It Your Way

Amen

Let the celebration begin!

STRONG WOMAN!

Your ◆ Queen!

I AM
What All Fear!

I AM
A Divine Sister Whose Destiny Is Near!

I AM
A Pillar Of Strength!

I AM
For In All Things I Give Thanks!

I AM
The Seed Of The Free!

I AM
And
Forever Will Be Somebody!

I AM
Mother Earth!

I AM
The Reason In Which You Were Granted Birth!

I AM
First!

I AM

The Nile That Quenches Your Thirst!

I AM

The Tune Which You Sing!

I AM

Liberty, Hear Me Ring!

I AM

What I Mean!

I AM

What I Seem!

I AM

All You Dream!

I AM

When Greeted

YOUR QUEEN!

La Diva

I am that queen

The one you dream for

I am more than the average woman.

You see, there's only one me

My self-worth is recognized

I can steal you with my cat eyes

Glowing

Thickness showing

Swaying left and right

A true vision that will drive a blind man to sight

There's no other

I am that mother

That nurturer that eases, that gives

Working hard so that my future generations may live

Get it right

I am that wife

That knows home is your peace of mind

Home is where you yearn to spend time

I am the freak

That you long to seek

Moves like waves

A heart of gold that never fades

I am

What I am

Diverse

A real conversation that never has to be rehearsed

I am first

Top of the line

Rare to find

Being me should be a crime

I am

What I am

For work was put in on me

So that you can witness what you see

The best has yet to come

Trust me

Now heed!

LA DIVA

Was born to succeed!

Jesus Is A Love Song

His unfailing love lasts forever long
Gentle yet free
God's Spirit touches all over and through me
All day and night
I shout Immanuel is my endless love, my
joy, my breath, my shining knight
I thank you my Sweetness my love of a lifetime
The reason for each of my rhymes
Because of You
I AM Me
A Child of God Raised By The Holy Trinity
Thank You Savior for Dying for Me on Calvary
For taking on all my sins and consequences that I embrace daily
When I think of Your Goodness my
whole body deep within shakes
I can't fake
You are the reason why God changed my fate
Here on Earth
Through you, in you, I find and walk into my true worth
You are worthy
The Great I AM That I AM
Ruler over this and all lands
Make your stand
And come through
For Lord, currently, we all need a Word from You
My Children Whom I so Dearly Love
Receive This Message from Above
It's all about Love!

It's all about giving thanks
To renew your strength
Prayer is the answer
Fasting is the key
Trust and unshakably believe
That now is truly your time has come
Praise Me for the Impossible, My Chosen One!
It Won't Be long!
All should know that

Jesus Is A Love Song!

It's Been A Long Time Coming But I Am Here!

**SISTER TRUTH SPEAKING THE TRUTH FOR
THE WORD OF GOD I DO COME TO SHARE!
LISTEN HERE!**

Old things are cast away and all things are anew
You Will Live to Love
You will rise in God's power from above
To speak out
Against the weaknesses of the flesh you will
no longer live in fear and self-doubt
The enemy's tricks
Living for material things and a quick fix
Is blocked
For you now knock
At the Lord's door
You now realize thank you Father for opening all eyes that
only through Jesus Christ, Son of God, do we obtain more!
We come
As God's Chosen Ones
To destroy negative thinking, actions, and words
The Truth
God's Words We Now Behold
God said, "That I come that you may have
life and have it more abundantly."
Did you hear that God himself is fighting for you and me!

Scripture says, "That this is the day that the Lord
has made we will rejoice and be glad in it!"
It's time to put down the violence, hear me for this was meant!
Our new day has come
God's voice and words shall reign across
this world my Chosen One
From this day forth we all shall declare and share!
IT'S BEEN A LONG TIME COMING, BUT I AM HERE!
Now go!
Pick up your bed and grow!

Move so that the Great I AM THAT I AM shows!

Praise Me For The Impossible!

PRAISE ME

For The Unattainable for The Unachievable

For The Unworkable for The Impractical

Praise Me for That Without a Solution

For The Time Has Come!

I Am That I Am

Will Be Known to Everyone!

Lord of Heaven's Armies!

Hallelujah!

My Creator That Formed Me!

Let Thy Will Be Done

Heaven Here On Earth Has Come!

For,

You

King of kings

Dwell amongst each and everyone

Right Now Come in Like a Flood

Cleanse All Sins with Your Blood

Father I Pray Continue to Give Us Your Unfailing Love

Your Unfailing Mercy

and Unfailing Grace!

For,

God We Pray

At The Day's End It's You Whom We Shall Embrace

Show Off in This Place

For I Am Blessed Coming In and Blessed Coming Out

No Weapon Formed Against Me Shall Prosper I Shout!

THE LORD SPEAKS

Yes, My Child You Are Beginning to See
That When You Praise Me
For The Impossible I Make It a Reality
I Am the Only Source That Can Fulfill Your Destiny
Question Is
When Are You Going to Believe?
Try Me and See If You Don't Succeed
Yet, You Have to Unshakably Believe
That What You Speak Shall Come

PRAISE ME FOR THE IMPOSSIBLE
MY CHOSEN ONE!

Faith Without Works Is Dead!

I Was Led
By The Holy Spirit to Speak This Word
May This Word Be Heard
By All!
Our Lord Said,
"Either You Serve Me Faithfully or You Fall!"
You see, I have to speak honestly
I said that I wanted to lose weight, but I continued
to eat the wrong things and late at night
I didn't exercise my faith right
You see,
I wanted, but I didn't want to change the old me!
I said that I wanted a house, but I didn't pay my bills
Credit shot
While surcharges were building up like hills
I said I wanted to start my own business, but I
dedicated no time to building the foundation
I said God will do the work if I just remain patient
I said that I was going back to school
I said that I was going back to church
But each time I couldn't keep my own
promises it really started to hurt!
I felt like a failure, I felt lazy, I felt confused
I wanted so badly by God to be used
To help make His Will be birthed
But my own lack of work
Kept me from living in my true worth
When I failed to labor for what I longed for

The more

Deeper into sin I fell giving glory to hell

But let me tell you something devil

Nothing just happens, this is all part of God's

design for my life this is why I was led

As a warning to say

Faith Without Works Is Dead!

Sometimes You Have to Encourage Yourself

To Be Your Better Self
Child,
If you don't get up and move into those
things that you were purposed to do
If you don't do right by you
Then who else will move in your favor
Stop trying to compare to your worldly neighbors
And grow!
Throw away all that mess that needs to go!
You know,
Those deadly deeds
Those sinful ways that you fulfill your needs
And believe
That the time has come
Don't you see many dying daily you better wake
up and surrender to God my Chosen One!
Use your common sense
You will lose your home if you don't pay the mortgage
You'll lose your car, without gas you won't go far
You'll lose your health if you fill yourself
up with junk, with poison smoke
If you don't swallow, you'll choke
This is meant
Child it's time to use your common sense!
And think hard before you just do

Just think how am I living before your
life on this Earth is through
Then where shall your Soul forever rest?
Child, don't do it if you can't give your best!
Stop settling for less!
And believe
That I was chosen to lead
That I am the head
Led by the Holy Spirit each day
Heed what I say
If you can't get it from anybody else!
Child,

SOMETIMES YOU HAVE TO ENCOURAGE YOURSELF!

Chapter 4

SINNERS HAVE SOUL TOO!

"For all have sinned and come short of the glory of God." (Romans 3:23 KJV)

"Instead of your shame there shall be a double portion;
instead of dishonor they shall rejoice in their lot;
therefore in their land they shall possess a double portion;
they shall have everlasting joy." (Isaiah 61:7 ESV)

"Let him know that whoever brings back a sinner from
his wandering will save his soul from death and will
cover a multitude of sins." (James 5:20 ESV)

"If we confess our sins, he is faithful and just to forgive us our sins
and to cleanse us from all unrighteousness." (1 John 1:9 ESV)

Don't Give Up On Yourself!

"Welcome Ms. Johnson, please have a seat."
I heard with big smiles as I entered
this anger management class
Which, by the way, if it wasn't for court I wouldn't be here
"So, Ms. Johnson, can you introduce yourself to the group?"
The instructor said as I rolled my eyes
Taking a deep breath
"My name is Shenail Johnson."
"Well, Shenail, can you tell us a little more about yourself?
Like your age, school, or where you live?" said the instructor
"Why?" I forcefully replied!
"I don't know nothing about you or anyone else up in here
So why should I share my goods?"
At that point everybody was looking
at me with a look of surprise
I rubbed my hands over my face taking another deep breath
"I grew up in Lakewood, the most dangerous part of the hood
I'm seventeen and a high school drop out!"
Well, after sitting 45 minutes listening to some
of the class members share their stories
I was ready to go!
So I stood up to leave
"Where are you going Shenail?" the instructor said
"Home!" Grabbing my coat
Then one of the other students sitting across from me said
"Don't leave don't give up on yourself!
Look, I know how it feels the first time you
have to address your problems.

It's not easy, girlfriend, it's terrifying!
But, I gave myself a chance. I sat down
after standing up just like you.
Trust me, my name is Samartha."
As she made her way over to me to reintroduce herself
I shook her hand and reluctantly sat back down in my seat
Samartha said, "Ms. Judy (our instructor's name)
I'm ready to share my deepest hurt,
the real source of my anger."
I sat there in amazement as this beautiful
young lady told us how
She was raped not once, not twice, but three
times by different family members,
Her boyfriend's friends, and her coach
She disclosed how she tried to commit suicide several times
And that her last time she was in the
state hospital for several months
She had six abortions and she was only sixteen!
She ran away from home and was caught selling drugs which
Finally placed her into this anger management class
And she hated herself
She felt as if she had nothing to live for

A tear fell down my eye and I looked
around and I noticed that the
Whole class was crying
Everyone had experienced some form of
hurt that brought on their anger
Samartha broke down screaming, "Why?"
screaming to the top of her lungs!

The instructor immediately grabbed
her and started holding her
Rocking her back and forth
It was her breakthrough, she finally released her pain, her hurt
"Now her healing process can begin," said the instructor
After ten minutes, Samartha calmed down and smiled
Making the whole class smile
I knew then that it was my time to release
I mean, I wanted to be able to smile like she did!
It's been so long since I smiled
During the moment of silence, I said aloud,
"My name is Shenail Johnson, and this is my story.
I was born in a prison, my mother was a heavy drug addict
And would do almost anything to feed her habit.
When I was 18 months old, my mother
gave custody of me to my uncle.
I was growing up in a positive environment. I had close friends,
food to eat, my own room, and I attended church every Sunday.
Well, May 19, 1994, my life turned for the worst.
My mother was released from prison and won custody of me.
I was ten years old when she moved into Mr.'s apartment.
Every day I would hear him beat her
call her all kinds of names,
And I never knew why this woman that I called my mother,
But I really didn't know her
I didn't remember her
Why?
Why would this woman allow herself to be abused every day?"
I wiped the tears from my eyes, cleared
my throat, and continued.

"He started abusing me when I turned around twelve.
He said that I was a woman now
And my mother knew it too!
He would give her drugs while she was
forced to watch him touch me!
I would scream for her, but she wouldn't even look at me!
I hated her, with a passion I hated them both!
I met this big-time drug dealer, and I ran away with him.
I was missing in action for 3 months.
Finally, I had to come back home."
Tears were falling heavily from my eyes
as everybody just watched me
I stood up,
"I loved him!
He was my hero, like a father that I never had.
He clothed and fed me, and made sure that I studied.
I was like a queen with him!

"Driving down the streets in his fancy car,
He stopped at a light and out of nowhere three guys
Started shooting at the car.
I turned to him only to witness a bullet
burst open the left side of his brain
Shots in his neck, chest, and arms while
his eyes were looking at me.
I screamed and then I was hit!
When I woke up, my mother and Mr. were both looking at me.
As the doctor called my mother out to explain that I was
Hit near my kidney, but was in stable condition,
Mr. came close to me and slapped me in the face.

Grabbing me by my ear, whispering, "Girl
don't you ever leave me again!"
It took me five months to fully heal from my wounds,
But till this day, I still miss my long lost love.
I was fifteen when my world was filled with every kind of sin.
I mean I slept around with almost anyone,
even women, man I just didn't care.
I smoked almost every kind of drug.
I was like Samartha, I had no self-love, no self-respect,
Anything destructive to me, to my
health, to my life, I would do it,
But I still couldn't die!
I even thought that if I got even with Mr.,
it could heal some of my pain,
But killing him didn't help!
It just landed me in jail.
I fought so much in there, man I got all kinds of scars.
Just look at this one across my face,
And all this frustration landed me into
this anger management class
And
I'm angry! I'm angry at the world!"
I didn't know that others had experienced
what I had to experience in life;
I always thought that I was by myself.
Samartha walked over to me and said, "Shenail, you are
no longer by yourself. You have a family within us."
And you know what, I did!
Now at the age of 21, I found a peace that
nobody could ever give me.

I found the Lord!
I surrendered all my pain
I released all my shame
And you know what? I'm so proud of myself!
I graduated from Temple University in Criminal Law.
It's my will to fight for those lost Souls
that fall beneath the cracks,
Lost Souls just as I was once lost,
I guess, the only thing that I can say is
what Samartha, my best friend,
Once said to me, "Don't Give Up On Yourself,"
Don't be afraid of what's new,
Most Importantly, my reader or listener,
Love all of you!
Amen!
Let your new life begin!

Mother To Daughter

Little girl,
Pull up a chair and listen as I share my world
To you
I pray these words are true
My sisters this poem is dedicated to you!

I grew up a dreamer
I guess reality was hard to accept, hard to live by
So, I lived my life as a lie
I yearned for attention, for attention made me
I judged my self-worth by what others see
My body matured before my mind
I was a dime piece
That all brothers wanted from north, south, west, and east
Hugs, I constantly embraced
Ballers all up in my face
So, I dated this guy
Man did he keep me high
Smoking all day, having his way with me
Feeling all on my body
You know, I didn't allow myself to have
a childhood, man did I run
Everyday doing nothing but having fun
Running those streets
Falling in and out of love with the guys I meet
Wondering is it hurt that I seek?
You know, many people tried to steer me right
Yet, I was grown and in control of my life!

They couldn't understand my ways of thinking,
Faking like they'd been there
Telling me their life stories as if I really care!
Little girl,
Do you feel that way?
Am I boring you or are you feeling what I say?
I'm going to continue anyway
I wanted to be loved, living the perfect life
A husband, big house, two kids, and having sex every night
What I'm about to say is deep
So, don't sleep!
I dropped out of high school, tenth grade, following some fool
Saying he was going to take care of me
Seven months pregnant, my eyes didn't want to believe
My man in our bed with my best friend!
I caught him cheating six times before our
relationship finally came to an end!
Leaving me more incomplete, more confused
Thinking,
Was I placed on this Earth to be used?
I think I damaged my child,
I was young, I still wanted to have fun and run wild!
Fussing and cussing all loud,
Exposing my child to the wrong things and negative crowd
No faking, it was my childish thinking!
Each night, I cried or stayed high to ease the pain
Suicidal thoughts, my mind was going insane
I was heading to a bottomless pit, selling my body for a fast fix
For ten dollars I would suck a man quick!
I want you to believe what I have to say

My life turned for the better in just one day!

Walking by, searching for my high

I read a sign, "Church doors are opening"

So, I walked in hoping to steal some cash

In and out of the collection basket real fast

But the pastor's words hit me deep, as

if he was talking just to me!

Saying, "It's time to sweep away the dirt."

Man, did his words hurt!

Then it came,

Church doors are open!

I closed my eyes, suddenly I felt my body rise

Walking to the front where the pastor awaits

With one hug my body started to shake

He touched my forehead and said,

"My child you are not a mistake, your destiny is yours to take!"

My burdens felt lifted, I was forgiven that day

And I pledged to live a new way

It sure wasn't easy, yet I survived

Five years later and I'm still not getting high!

I lost many friends, for they were still motivated by sin

I even took a breather from men

It was my goal to win!

I lived to be loved

Yet,

Love will never come unless it lies within you first!

The love of self you must thirst for!

My little girl,

My daughter,

Be more than me!

Live your life and strive to be

All you can be

I paid the price

So that you can live right

Mommy's just saying

Love Your Life!

This Is True,

Nobody Is Going to Love You

Like You Love You!

Here's A Clue

YES,

I'M TALKING TO

YOU!

MOTHER TO DAUGHTER

No More Strife!

DEAR SISTERS, DEAR FRIENDS
Free your minds and let me in
This is where the new you begins

Satan is busy trying to attack the part of you that is weak!
Preying on the sinners that he can seek!
GOD
Is sending us a word
"ABSTINENCE"
Is what I heard!
I know what you are thinking
No, it's not that easy
Yet, it's not that hard
When you surrender and allow GOD to be in charge!
I was baptized as a child
Yet, I knew not the true meaning of this event

MY SISTERS
It's time to repent!
And
Be washed again in the blood of CHRIST
Sending those sins back to the owner
And
Walking into your new life!
You tried it your way
Living day by day with unfulfilled dreams

MY SISTERS

It's not as hard as it seems
Yet, You Must Surrender
Yet, You Must Let Go
Yet, You Must Be Obedient To GOD
Yet, His Words You Must Know!

It's time the war inside of you has reached its peak
It's time to strengthen that, which is weak!
And
Tell the Devil you can't have this body!
You can't steal my mind!
You can't corrupt my soul!
For, I have strengthened my defense with
JESUS who makes me whole!

MY FRIENDS

The plague of Aids is killing us
Stop satisfying your flesh
And
Giving that man your life and trust!
If he really loves you
Then marriage is not a conversation, but is true
We all know the old saying, "Why buy
the cow if the milk is free?"
It's time to live for you & strive to be all you can be
I Pray
The New You Must Start Today & Say

NO MORE STRIFE!

SEX WITHOUT MARRIAGE, TAKING NEGATIVITY, RUSHING LIFE, IRRESPONSIBLE THINKING, FAKE RELATIONSHIPS, AND EATING AWAY MY SOUL!
Pray for balance and self-control, then be
still for God will make you whole!

Grandma's Teachings

MY GRANDMA

Once said,

"That if a man can't stand to be seen with you at day

Then he doesn't deserve the privilege to be with you at night!"

And

Let me tell you my sisters

Grandma usually knows what's right!

I'm calling on my sisters

Because I know that you will understand

When you think you had a gift sent from heaven

A gift you called your man!

Who turned your joy into pain!

Steadily driving your mind insane!

Who turned your smiles into frowns!

An everlasting roller coaster

Constantly heading down!

Well,

Enough is enough!

You see,

The new millennium is here!

And

This phenomenal woman

Can no longer bear

This nonsense!

Pay close attention to this!

I would rather be alone

Than have a low-life man claiming to be my own!

You see,

MY GRANDMA

Instilled in me

That I only deserve the best!

And

GOD as my witness

I will not settle for any less!

He Said He Loved Me

He said he cared
He said that he would always be there
So, I gave all of myself
I dedicated my life to him and no one else
I cooked, I cleaned
I provided so that he wouldn't want for anything
I was his woman, proud as can be
I was his woman
Yet, he didn't return the same love to me
I grew satisfied with less
I slowly found myself constantly moody and depressed
One day I finally realized that my own dreams were covered up
I felt stuck
In a situation where I put myself last
Now, how am I going to survive without enough cash?
I don't want to be lonely, yet am afraid that if I stay
That I will live a lie for the rest of my life every day
I'm not special, I just want to survive
I'm not more than you!
Yet,
I must stand and strive!
I must step out on faith
And
Allow GOD to direct my strength!
There's nothing to fear but fear itself
This time
I'm dedicating my life to me and no one else!
Yes,

I might get lonely, but I'm never alone
Yes,
I may not have anyone to talk to, but GOD hears my every tone
I'm no more special than you, just an ordinary girl
Yet,
This is my world to take!
To you that reads remember GOD doesn't make mistakes!
There's a reason why you were granted life
Now,
Tell yourself the reasons why you should choose right!
It's your time to shine
You go girl!
Make your mark on this world!
NOW MOVE!
Get people out of your way
Smile for today is a new day!

YOU SEE,
NO MORE HE SAID HE LOVED ME!

Constructive Criticism

Constructive means helping to develop or improve something.
Criticism means fault-finding.
So this is faultfinding to help develop and improve you.
Can I come through?

Lord teach me through this pen
Allow your wisdom to flow so that I might win
Now let us begin

My name I shall not reveal for this story is true
I'm only speaking out because you still
have a chance to save you

I grew up in a stable home
Having five brothers and two sisters never
left me with a chance to be alone
My life turned for the worst in 2003
I mean I completely lost a piece of me
Here's it
A day that I will never forget

It started out like an ordinary day
Mom's yelling at me to wake up for school
As I place the pillow over my head to
block out the words she says
Then here comes the slamming of my door
"Boy get up!" Mom you don't have to yell no more!
Damn school,

Half of my class only goes there to act a fool!
Normal, hurry up, I have to use the bathroom bad
Man, I'll be glad
When I get out this house
And bounce
In my own crib
There I can live free
"Mom, I'm coming. Stop rushing me!"

Get in class
Hoping these periods go fast
I got things to do
Hook up and run with my crew
Later
Then comes in Mr. Smith who I classified as a hater
He is speaking about something
But I'm not listening to what he calls his positive speech
Yelling just like my mom about improving in you what is weak
Mr. Andrew, what do you think he said?
I looked up dumbfounded placing my hands on top of my head,
"What?"
"What do you think about constructive criticism?"
He said as he led his way near my seat.
"I don't know can you repeat
What you were talking about?"
As he shouted to the class,
"If you follow in this young man's footsteps,
you'll always finish last."
"What!" I said, "Go ahead with that."
Go ahead with that

Now that doesn't make any sense
My young brother, learn how to properly speak
Man, I stood to my feet
And stepped up right in his face
I said, "Is this proper enough?" as my fist hit his face!
I couldn't believe that I hit my own teacher,
as he grabbed me down to the floor
Oh no, I thought, now I'm in trouble for sure
The principal called my father, but he
was out in the field doing sales
Then he called my mother. All hell
Here she goes again
I'll bet she'll be yelling
Man, this drama will never end
I heard them pleading with my mother to come pick me up
Yet my mother kept telling them I'm stuck
At work
Look, I'll see what I can do.
I sat in that office for two hours straight
Man, I thought to myself, why is my mother so late?
Then my dad rushed in with a worried
look that I never saw before
My little brothers and sisters followed him through the door
"Son, get your belongings your mother was hit!"
"What!" I stood up yelling in a fit!

We arrived at the hospital. My relatives and
grandmother were already there.
I could hear
The tears before we made it to the waiting room

My uncle hugged my dad and said she didn't make it through!

I couldn't breathe. My mother is dead? No, this ain't true!

"Let me through let me through!"

I ran to her room

But they wouldn't let me in

I felt like l was dreaming a nightmare that wouldn't end

Yet it's true

My young sister hit me yelling, "Mommy's dead because of you!

You just had to be difficult, you just couldn't do what was right!

My mommy's dead because you couldn't control your life!

Why!

Why!"

As my dad grabbed her back off me,

"Son, you can't blame yourself, trust me!"

There it goes again, I couldn't breathe

I just had to leave

So I ran out to the streets

I didn't even look at the crack in the

sidewalk as I fell off my feet

Face first

I shouted, "Mommy, it's me, not you, who

should be surrounded by dirt!"

I had a hurt

That I never felt before

I only wished that I could turn back the

hands of time and strive for more!

Why didn't I just listen? Why couldn't I accept the truth!

All people were telling me was to treasure my youth!

But, I had to do me

Constructive criticism was just disciplining
me to be and strive for all I can be
Here I stand over top of my mother's grave
Telling this story to you to change so that
your loved one's life may be saved
You
Don't be a fool, for this story is true
I lost
My negative attitude cost
Me my pride and joy
You see, no more
Mommy's Little Boy!

Father To Son

MY SON,

I asked your mother for this visit

I'm sorry that we have to talk through this glass

Man, my little boy has grown up so fast

I missed so much in your life

I only wish that I could correct the wrong right

Yet, I choose to live my life in strife

You see,

School just wasn't for me

I didn't pay attention

My negative attitude and jokes kept me in detention

I didn't do my work, constantly cutting class

Chasing behind some girl until time passed

Smoking weed

Started getting money to fulfill my needs

I didn't know

That the road I was traveling was the wrong place to go

Is that it?

Nothing personal, but dad I didn't come to hear this

You had it brought

You got sloppy so you got caught

Oh, so you think I'm in jail over drugs.

Selling on the corners like your local thugs?

Oh, no!

Shut up and listen before your hard head go!

I can see,

Talking to you was like talking to the childish me!

Living for each day, not being exposed to a higher way

I'm a murderer, my son

Killing punks like you just for fun

Why sell when you can rob

Take the goods while your determined self does the job

I killed so many people, now I can hardly sleep

Every time I close my eyes a demon I meet

I had it all, never thinking one day that I could fall on my face

Now hell chases my inner being

I mean

I can't lie

I'm thinking my time is near to die

The preacher said, "My lost brother, please use your head

Give your life to Christ."

Yet, how can He forgive me when every

day I did wrong, not right?

When I get high

I start thinking about suicide

I hate it in here!

I hate that every day I have to watch my back in fear!

Man, these dudes just don't care!

28 years

28 years I lost

All because I wanted to be down and floss

To say I am my own boss!

Son!

I was wrong!

My whole outlook on life was wrong!

I can't take people selling this fantasy like
gang banging makes you strong!
I just wanted us to meet
I just wanted to see your face
Before death I embrace

Dad, wait!
Maybe what the preacher said can change your fate!
It's been hard out here
Not having a father to share my pain
I, too, sometimes feel like I'm going insane
Mom,
Walked up and gave her life to Christ
Ever since then she has been living a joyful life
I hear her pray
Maybe if we do, we both will be forgiven today

Son,
I never prayed before
I wouldn't even know what to ask Him for

Mom,
I saw her grab the other person's hand and bow their heads
I think I can repeat some of the words they said

Son,
Then touch my hand on the glass, close
your eyes, and bow your head
Now go repeat what she said
"My gracious Father of all high

Hear our supplications and sorrowful cry

I believe that you died for our sins

I believe with Jesus we shall win

In the Name of Jesus

Forgive us, save us, grow us, touch us, for we need your healing

We need your rebuilding love

Our provider, our friend, our protector from above

Order our steps, show us what is next to claim in Jesus' Name

We pray,

Amen."

Dad you can raise your head now

Dad! Dad!

Do you hear me?

Dad! What's wrong?

Guards, what's wrong with my Father?

He's not moving

He's not moving!

For a fact,

Just like that

While we were praying my father was stabbed in his back

That day was my turning point

His death brought me life

My father was just trying to tell me to live right

To keep God's insight

This is why I write

This is why I speak

I can't get back what's 6ft deep

My father,

Who wanted so much to relive

Who wanted so much not to take, yet to give

As for him, I too was forgiven by Christ
And I guess my message for this story is that
it's never too late to change your life
It's never too late
To labor in that which will alter your fate
Stop it! I heard what you said
I can't believe you even allowed that
thought to enter into your head
Why don't you believe
That you were granted this life, this moment to succeed
As we were born, death too awaits
Just Remember
One thing
My People
It's Not Too Late!
STRIVE
DO OR DIE!

A
Lost Son

I could have been anyone
Yet, I chose defeat when I fell in love with the streets
I just had to be down
To floss
To call myself my own boss throughout my town
Yet, I'll tell you the truth
Every day was an internal battle between
right and wrong, my youth
Like so many other falling soldiers, I didn't make it through
You know, I truly didn't care about life
until I was faced with death
I honestly thought that I could overcome
any threat brought to me
But death became my only reality
Here it is, I want you to visualize this

Like any other night I was making my rounds
Just got down on the smoke
Hanging with my boys, you're bound to choke
Then out of nowhere came my worst fear 5-O
Yo, I knew that I was packing so I had to go
I took off running through the dark alley ways, jumping gates,
Running all through people's places
I looked back to see if I had lost the police
Then my cell phone rang, it was from my niece
Not seeing the cops in sight, I decided to answer my phone

"What!" My niece said, "Your mom
said it's late. Come on home!"
I told her, "Tell my mother when I feel like
it, but for now just leave me alone!"
And I hung up
Stuck in an unfamiliar place
I thought to myself man it's hot out here
I know that one of my boy's cribs is near
Yeah, that's where I'll go
Smoke, chill, and lay low
As I turned the corner
I saw one of my old peeps driving by
I yelled out, "Man, can I get a ride to the south-side?"
He said, "Yeah my man get in!"
So, I did, even though my boy had three other dudes in the
car. I didn't care, just as long as I had peace of mind.
Underneath I felt happy that I didn't get
caught and have to do time
The dude in the front asked me, "If I was Thomas's
boy, Thomas McKnight from the west-side?"
I said, "Yeah, I know Thomas."
He said, "I know you were with his boys
when they stole my man's car."
Right then and there I thought to myself, "Get out of this car.
You don't have to walk too far; it's only up eight streets."
That dude turned around and said, "I knew
one day that we would finally meet."
He told my boy driving, "It's time to prove your loyalty!"
As I was trying to jump out of the moving car, my
old boy quickly stopped the car and shot at me.

I was moving so fast that I didn't even notice that I was shot

Eventually, I dropped to the ground

It was so late at night that nobody could be found

I couldn't breathe

The last thing I heard, "Man, I hear 5-O we got to leave!"

Then bang!

A shot straight to my head

Those dudes just left me out to the dead

I couldn't move, tears were coming from my eyes

I thought about my mother. I could just hear her cries!

Blood

Lying in a puddle of blood

I thought about my love for the streets

How it left me out on my own. That quick

cash was my ultimate defeat

I felt so cold

I could just feel the chills deep in my bones

I was so used to being surrounded by

others, but now I'm left alone

Blood was coming out of my mouth

when the ambulance arrived

I prayed, "Please don't let this be my time to die!"

Then, my eyes closed

I was heading to a place where nobody knows

19

19, filled with talents and big dreams

Never to come true

I'm only speaking out because you still

have a chance to save you!

All that glitter and gold

Is not worth your soul

It's not worth your life

I promise you - selling your soul to the devil

is filled with murder and strife

Yeah right,

I know what you're thinking

Man

I thought the same, never me!

Yet, I told you before playing in hell,

death will be your only reality

I wish, but it's too late

I wish that I had the chance to change my fate!

Why didn't I listen?

Why did I just have to do me?

I could have been anyone, now death I see

I remember, what my mother said

Now I see that it's true

Nobody is going to love you more than you!

I plead,

Grow to be anyone

But another Lost Son

Tell yourself right now, "I Am Someone!"

Well,

I had my short time!

FLATLINE!

Say This Prayer:

Lord,

I need you now more than ever

To change my sinful ways before I'm lost forever
Come in like a storm
Lord, keep me, make me strong!
I've strayed away
It's not You only me Lord who shall pay
Yet, I can't survive another day
Lost in this endless circle, this death trap,
this hell hole that I created
Lord, I hate it
But I can't do this by myself
Lord, I know that only You can help me grow to be somebody else
I now believe
Lord, let your living Word cling
You see,
I'm not a lost son. I Am Someone!
Amen
Let My Restoration Begin

It Starts At Home

Your child is a reflection of you
They mimic the words you say and the things you do
Therefore, the healing must begin first with you
Raising your child doesn't mean giving them
material things or items you once longed for
Dear mother and father, it causes much more
The answer is simple - put your child first
What you hold as important, they will thirst
It's your judgment to their means of satisfaction
Stop accepting their negative behaviors and actions
Stop feeding into instant gratification
There's no ease through the storm, you must remain patient
Oversee your child as overseers watched their owner's slaves
Know everything they do, who they're
hanging out with, and talking to
Grab ahold before the fouls of the street sores through
All I can say is when and why?
When was the last time that you visited your child's school?
Come on parents, you should know that knowledge is the tool
Why is your child failing, acting a clown,
and disrespecting their teachers?
Oh, it's easy to blame the teachers, like man
expecting no sin from the preachers
If you know the answer, then why haven't they changed?
Is it that your authority lies at a short range?
Get Your House In Order
Place Focus Where Focus Needs To Be
Don't get defensive, just hear me!

For the time is now, the war has reached its peak

My child, it's time to feed your soul in

order to remain strong, not weak

Life is granted to serve, to sacrifice, and to

give others all the love that they deserve

Your seed was planted to grow in the righteousness of My Name

THE LORD SPEAKS

It is I that they must seek!

Dedicate your time to live right. Pray for insight.

Or like a thief in the night death will steal your life

Then where shall you lay?

The test was determined by how you lived each day

Fight against evil before he encompasses

you, then through your seeds

The weapons lie within. I have granted you all you need.

The Victory Is Yours

For the devil is already defeated!

IT STARTS AT HOME

HEED IT!

We Are At War!

Lord I pray,
Grant me the words to say to reach all people today

I have to speak as if these are my last words
Listen up for this knowledge must be heard
You were born for a reason
Like the seasons that come and go
Your last day, no one knows
You must pray for strength to change
You must deny yourself to serve others
You must respect your sisters and brothers!
We're living in a time of jealousy and hate
A time where no one wants to give, but take
A time where negativity crowds the street
Where people cling to that which makes them weak!
For love, for justice, for equality, I will die
Then live my life as a lie!
What!
No one can change this world until they change themselves
Stop worrying about everyone else!
What they said, what they wear, or the color of their face
It's up to you, my army, to embrace!
I must pause for this moment cause for a deeper touch
You see,
It's time to embrace us!
It's time to appreciate, time to dedicate our lives
It's time to live right!
Like a hawk preying on the dead, our souls must be fed

I see a frown, let me break this down

There's a war going on inside of each of us

A battle between two wolves

One is evil, one is good

The evil wolf is fed by anger, hatred, and deceit!

Its sole purpose for living is to keep you weak, to steal your joy

Having mothers crying over the dead bodies of their little boys

The good wolf is fed by love, peace, and self-control!

Its sole purpose for living is to make you whole, to serve

To sacrifice and give others all the love that they deserve

Then love will be returned unto you keep it real, stay true!

Who shall win the final battle you say?

Ask yourself, which wolf do I feed today?

The War Has Reached Its Peak

Starve the evil and the good wolf you must long to seek!

Remember,

Life is not to waste!

If you don't believe me, ask the dead

Oh, you can't

I rest my case!

WE ARE AT WAR!

If I'm Gonna Speak
I'm Taking It Straight
To The Streets

I grew up in a broken home

My mother's drug habit left me as a child to survive on my own

Middle school hit

That's when I got tired of this broke mess for real

If I wanted to fit in with the popular crowd,

all name brand stuff I had to steal

I got caught numerous times

My Earth would sell whatever was left behind

Saying

Next time I'll leave your stupid self in jail

Who do you think paid your bail fee?

Yes, your mommy

Now give me whatever drugs you got

I need to hit up the spot

To feel good

I tell you, life ain't worth nothing living in the hood

So I thought

Until one day I was brought

In front of this gang leader

Talking about, I'm a breeder of money!

Man I'll have you filthy rich before you even turn twenty!

What!

That's just what I needed to hear

Yo, I did whatever, I just didn't care

I stole cars, I sold drugs

I even killed some punks claiming to be thugs
By the age of twenty
People were calling me Money
I was his lieutenant
Most loyal soldier in the street
Man, I could have any female I meet
My game was tight
I had a bad Benz that I called midnight
I'll never forget
Walking down an alleyway, watching my mom beg for that hit
For the first time, I felt so sad
For my own Earth was out there bad
I think back to when it all began
Yeah, when she let that no good man in
She started missing working chasing behind him with the next
And all he wanted from her was a place to stay, cash, and sex

I used to hear them get high
Every time I used cry
Because he would start hitting her and raping her
I could just hear her scream
I would close my eyes and try to sleep a positive dream
When he left her for her best friend
That's when her drug habit truly kicked in
There I watched her on her knees
Begging, I'll go down on you please
No more of this I flipped
I couldn't believe that one of my main peeps would
let my mom disrespect herself for a hit
I rode up on him quick

Bang, bang!

Straight to the heart

My mom started to run, I just couldn't accept the fact

She looked at me and turned and I shot her in the back

I heard someone coming so I bounced

I brought an ounce

Of haze

Sat back in the chair in a daze

What did I do?

Who am I!

I screamed!

I have no clue

The phone rang

It was the gang leader

He said, "Yo!

Meet me at the place, there's something I most know!"

That sounded wack

I knew that I would have to come strapped

When I arrived

All my peeps looked like somebody has to die

I cleared my head

As the leader said

Yo, Tommy was shot in the heart

I guess those puck bloods want to start

A war for sure

You strapped?

I said, "My man, you know that."

We piled up into the car

Their hang out spot wasn't far

I kept telling myself

Yo, tell them the truth

Before we go murder some innocent youth

But if I tell them that then I'll be dead

Man, play it safe and use your head

We rode up on the spot, the window went down

Man, they shot and killed everyone found

I couldn't move

Look what I started - a blood war

Retaliation will come for sure

"Move," my man said

As he shot this little girl in the head

He yelled, "Go to hell. Tommy was my best man!

None of you punks will be able to stand."

Again

We rode off into the wind

I heard a noise when we returned to our spot

It was crack-head Joan talking about man the streets are hot

The gang leader said, "What are you doing here?"

"I got some information to share.

It's about your boy, Tommy. You care to hear?"

Man, we shot those punks dead

What! You started the war!

No, they did use your stupid head!

What! Tommy's death was an inside job

He grabbed up Joan by her shirt and put a gun to her face

And said, "You'd better speak before your life I rob!"

It was Midnight!

I saw it with my own eyes as he took

Tommy's and his own mother's life

What!

Those dudes ever turned so fast
I dashed to the door
"Bang, bang," suddenly I hit the floor
Man, you got us all killed
I faintly heard
As gun shots from nowhere were heard
It was the bloods shooting to kill
While the focus was off of me
I crawled towards a hole where no one could see
I watched all my friends die
One at a time
I'm breathing at an irregular pace
I knew death I would eventually embrace
Then a strange voice appeared
It drew near
No faking
Lying right next to me was Satan
"Well done
My Son
I knew for materialistic things
You would do something strange
Just to be down
Just to be well known and respected
throughout this hell-hole town."
My evil knight
You even took your own mother's life
What God placed in her could have destroyed my whole army
I just couldn't kill her, but you did
Now my face no longer has to be hidden
War War War!

My army is growing stronger over this nonsense for sure!
Well, enough talk
I've got things to do
Take your last breath. Death got the best of you
Suddenly
I heard another loud voice
It said, "Samuel you have a choice to live
Yet, your soul to me you must give."
My eyes opened towards a bright light
My auntie standing over top of me whispered,
"God has spared your life."
I was in recovery for five months and three days
Yo, I did a 360. I completely changed my old ways
I moved to a new state
I faithfully attend church and allow God to direct my fate
I'm speaking out to you
Now is the time to recognize what is true
Heaven or Hell
Triumph or fail
No more
I want to succeed in life for sure
The question is
What about you?
Are you still living in darkness, stay true?
Please don't allow death to get the best of you
Don't be afraid to move ahead
Don't be afraid to cut off negative friends
Don't be afraid to let the new you in Christ begin
This is why my spirit was not put to rest!
I had to tell you, my people,
Stop settling for less!

Can I Tell My Story?

Gathering My Thoughts
Now, Where Shall I Start?

It started out with weed
Back then that was all I needed to get high
Sit back, eat, and laugh until I cry
Oh, I used to act a fool!
Working on the block while skipping school
On the real, my teachers were wack!
Always trying to get a brother to improve his act
Then it happened, I caught my first case
Police riding up on a brother with mace
My Earth broke down
Wasn't really worrying about me, but it
hurt to see her disappointed frown
So, I stayed out of trouble for awhile
Messed up and had a child
A male soldier
Named him after me
Keeping it real, his birth brought out the best in me
For a moment
The blocks called and I was on it!
Come on,
I had a child to feed
I didn't want to be like my father. I was
going to take care of my seed
School didn't pay
That early time was taking away my money

Learning what? When I'm out here flipping twenties!
Man,
Then it happened again
My second drug charge with a large bail fee
Money stack fell short
Yo, this game was getting the best of me!

I'll never forget
That was the day my Earth smacked me
in the face in front of crowd
Screaming all loud
About how I'm acting like my father
repeating his negative ways
Thinking to myself, "Whatever you say."
I started hanging out more with my boys
Dipped the weed,
At that point a stronger high I needed to get by the day
Third charge, this time I got sent away
Yo, some crazy things happened to me in jail!
I started analyzing where I failed short in life
I never really listened to those who tried to steer me right!
I thought back to what my mother said
About my father and how I was following in his footsteps
I thought about my seed. Will it hit him next?
Man, I'm not even around to take care of him
I guess that's how the cycle begins
It did for me; my dad I would never see!
I found myself feigning for drugs to wash the pain away
Its hunger grew stronger each day!
By the time I saw the streets, I was a full-blown crack head

Hell and darkness my journey led!

People saying,

"This can't be true, James I know that's not you!"

Man, things got really bad

Eating out of the garbage and sleeping

on the street drove me mad!

Then my worst nightmare happened

I saw my seed

Sitting on the park bench with his friends smoking weed!

It reminded me when my dad saw me smoking

Walked up, I started choking

I yelled at him,

"Man, you haven't been in my life all this time.

Don't you dare tell me how to do right,

In anger I almost whipped out my knife!"

So, I did nothing

Just walked by

Felt lower than a failure

Man did I get high!

That last hit

I hit the floor

Feeling dizzy, trying to make it to the door!

My body wouldn't move

Air couldn't get through

The game appeared and said I got the best of you!

No faking

Standing over top of me was Satan!

I had you believe

That you couldn't achieve in school

Fool
You should have listened to your teachers
You should have walked up when the preacher called you home
Now,
No one can hear your tone!
You denied your mother of her most sacred joy
The life of her little boy!
You left your seed
Just like your father left you
By the way,
Thanks. He'll do right
Another ignorant brother without sight
Another lost man
Hard-headed, lack of discipline, and too confused
To stand
On his own two feet
This battle between man
Is becoming too easy to seek and defeat
Just Like You!
Don't Pray to God Now
When Everyday He Knocked
You Wouldn't Let Him Through!
Say Good Night to Your Fans
DEATH GOT THE BEST OF YOU!
STORY TOLD!

Yo!

I want you to see the world through my eyes
No sugar coating or telling lies
Let me share my silent cries

Street Life
Yo, I was born into this
Slick talking, people getting hit daily
I swear to thee
Hell only been my life story, before the change
Now, this might be strange
But at the age of twelve I fell into sin
Okay, this is where the story begins

My first job was as a lookout
I can remember my O'G saying, "Boy if
you see 5-O you better shout
Don't doubt that if you mess up your life won't be taken out!"
So, I did what I had to do
Stealing cars, selling drugs, killing grimy
thugs, and robbing people just like you
But I made it through to see my riches grow
But I kept thinking that I could only succeed
by building on the things I know
Yo, many people warned me that this street
life had to go like my brother
Now, this is going to hurt
Just mentioning his name makes me think
about him six feet under the dirt
Caught up in the game, always striving for fame

But, what did it get him?
Yo, if you knew my brother, you would say
that he was born to win in life
But on the real, every day for him was filled with strife
Always having to watch his back
Having to accept the fact that you can't trust
anyone, not even your own family
I tell you misery was his only reality
Six times straight to the heart, three shots straight to the head
I tell you, those punks really did want my brother dead
You know, that's where the change began
I always remembered my big brother telling me to grow
to be someone different than what you daily see
Grow to be anyone but me
He said that this road that I travel leads to a dead end
It's like a lost cause for the lost souls of
children, women, and men
Don't take that road, let your dream begin
Yeah, that's where it did
I released the gifts that I so often hid
I finished school
Yo, they weren't lying when they said that knowledge
is the tool that unleashes your mind
Question is: How long are you going to waste your time?
Procrastinating, so focus on those that are hating
Dating sinful mates, too lazy to change your fate!
Get up and move, don't think, just do
Yo, you know what I'm saying is true
In other words, stop doing you
Let that mess go
YO!

Sweet Sixteen

SWEET SIXTEEN WAS THE YEAR FOR ME!
New people, slamming parties
I even lost my virginity
I lived for their looks, like a chain my
body hooked their attention
Their curiosity runs wild
On the real, they didn't even care if I was a child
It was his slick words, thuggish ways, and
brown eyes that made me lie
Cut school, for his love I would act like a fool
Turn around, another girl in his face
Thinking, these chicken heads are going
to force me to use my mace
Then it happened,
11:10 in the morning the doctor did say that I was HIV positive
Hell no, no way!
Top it, that's not the worst
You're 3 months pregnant. My heart nearly burst!
LIFE?
I thought I knew all the answers, I was handling me
I wasn't prepared for this tragedy
Hard as a rock, yet the tears melted down my face
I never thought that I could get the death case
Dazed, feeling trapped in a maze
So, the doctor suggests
That I call this group home they're supposed to be the best
Step in my complex, I see the locals getting high
I think, why me? Why can't one of them die?

The phone rings
Hello,
Oh shorty, I can't come over. I got somewhere to go
Sweetie, hold on, there's something you should know
Tell me later, I got to go!
That night I felt so alone
Trapped in a tomb, screaming yet nobody could hear my tone
I dreamed of the woman I was supposed to be
Strong, positive, and intelligent making
my goals become a reality
Yet, I rushed
Rushed to be loved because I thought love, loved me
Showing all my body
Allowing people to touch my most sacred parts
Now, where are they when my heart slowly starts to beat?
My breathing is becoming weak
My eyes close,
An overdose of pills has me heading to
a place where nobody knows
My life came to an end
Before it even had a chance to begin
Yet, my Spirit would not rest until these words were heard
Love you!
Love every particle that makes you, You!
Live your life to the fullest, for death is true
Every decision you make
A consequence follows, so please take time to debate
I pray you choose right
For, the wrong choice cost me my life!
October 10, 2002

My Seventeenth Birthday
I'M ONLY SORRY THAT I COULDN'T
SHARE IT WITH YOU!
SWEET SIXTEEN

City Slick

Whipping those sisters with my killer stick
Polluting with each hit
Pay close attention to this

Getting women came as quickly as losing cash on the streets
That thug that your family prayed you wouldn't meet
Is here
Can somebody pass the weed before I share my goods?
The chaos that's encompassing our hoods
Now my head is right
Let me tell you about that night
It started out as an ordinary day
Same old people that passed my way
Then a breath of fresh air
This bad sister was walking near me
By the end of the night, she'll be calling me Daddy
Mack Daddy pulled out all the cards
As we walked across the yards
To her girlfriend's house
Plans was set - 8:30 we would bounce
A brother prepared for the night
Brought some drinks an ounce of haze
Sitting in the car
Hotel not far
I started caressing on her soft, smooth legs
Open the room door
It was on for sure
Hit the bed

Sister bent down to give me some head

I rushed those legs up in the air

Yo, a brother ran up in her without a condom. I just didn't care

Screaming my name

I knew that this body I would claim

As my own

Smoking on the bed, then I heard my phone

It was my boy Chill

Man, I just heard. Don't mess with that chick. Her sex kills!

What are you talking about!

AIDS, man, you better bounce!

We're going to the spot

I drop that phone

While her sexy self was lying on the bed alone

And out of frustration I yelled, "Chick!

Are you carrying that Aids hit?

You'd better tell me now before I leave

your body lying in a ditch!"

"What!

You didn't ask!

Anyway

You used protection you'll be okay!"

Man, what more can I say?

HIV positive still as today

Still sexing those bad chicks that come my way

City Slick

Infesting this world with my killer stick

Sisters you better meditate on this!

For, if you don't ask

I sure won't show

Same old mess people dying daily and don't even know

City Slick

Whipping those sisters with my killer stick

Polluting with each hit

Pay close attention to this!

Common Sense

I GUESS IT'S COMMON NOT TO USE YOUR SENSE
FOR, SO MANY DO
CAN I KEEP IT REAL? THIS POEM
IS DEDICATED TO YOU!

Common Sense, would have told you not to
smoke when you know death awaits
You, weak soldier leaving yourself open for Cancer's easy bait!
Common Sense, would have told you not to sleep
with a man you just met without a condom
I know the mood was right
Your weakness of the flesh cost you your life
Lying on your death bed, contemplating
was that moment worth it?
If only I could choose again
Quick thinking brought your life to an end!
Common Sense, would have told you that if
this person has too many have nots
Then why would you drop them drawers?
Wondering why they don't take care of their children
Well, you knew that before you gave it to the moron raw!
Common Sense, would have told you how
are you going to gain respect
Showing half or all your body parts?
One look at you and a sexual mindset starts
No! He's not thinking about marriage
He's thinking how quick can I hit, stick, or lick
You get the hint!

Common Sense, would have told you that your unpaid bills
Don't go away; surcharges building up like hills
Your credit is shot can't get a loan anywhere
Then to ease your mind you say I don't care!
Common Sense, would have told you that if you
were not happy with the person in the beginning
Then why would you marry them?
Oh, you settled, couldn't wait for your soul mate
Another quick decision that altered your fate!
Common Sense, would have told you that you don't
go to church when you get yourself together
But, that you go to church to get together
Not a quick fix, but a high that will last forever!
Common Sense, would have told me to use my Common Sense
And recognize that these words will not change
people's thoughts or their daily living
Yet, my Common Sense says keep on giving
Keep on preaching, keep on teaching
for you are reaching within
Now their healing may begin!
Where Common Sense recognizes that it takes Common Sense
To win in life!
My people we must strive to live right!
Don't block!
Don't put up your defense!
A SISTER'S JUST SAYING

USE YOUR
COMMON SENSE!

Fighting For My Life!

I grew up in a messed-up situation
Mom's getting high, Dad's never home
Without telling a long story, pretty much a
brother was left to fend for his own
I can't do this
I mean I can't tell about my life and
all the mess I was exposed to
I mean what was a seven-year-old supposed to do
When you're held down and constantly raped
I hate the thought
Growing up having problems maintaining
any kind of healthy relationships
With the drama of everyday living
Sinning became my daily routine
I mean
I just didn't care. I had no fear of dying.
Hell, I was living it!
No food, no lights, no clothes, no love, no support, no trust,
make a simple mistake and people start having a fit
But through it all
Man, I promised myself that I wouldn't fall
So, you know I tried to play it the right way
Trying to get the school thing on, making everything legit
But, I tell you I didn't truly know hell until I tried to quit
You know be a better me
Yet, with the mess in the streets topped with my own negative
attitude becoming a better person only seemed like a fantasy
You know,

That which I say I wouldn't do
I do
That which I do
I regret
I mean, I really feel like a loser because I
can't even keep promises to myself
So, here I am speaking to you, torn between two roads
Do I take the less traveled or where everyone else goes?
Do I follow what is familiar where I might have a
chance for success, or do I step out on faith?
Man, I'll confess
There's a fear, a lack of confidence and uncertainty
traveling the road only journeyed by few
I didn't want to accept what other teachers around me knew
That I can't fight this battle by myself
That there's a higher power, yet you
must surrender all of yourself
I know,
It flew over my head the first time I heard that too
Yet, keep living I promise that it will come to you!
You see,
It's an internal battle every day between wrong and right
And if you're listening to me now, I'll bet
that you too are fighting for your life!
Fighting to stay above all the negativity and nonsense
Fighting to control your temper and not
to be so quick to take offense
Fighting for a good life
Fighting to keep joy, peace, and wise insight
Yet,

If you didn't get anything from this pay attention to this truth
You have to first join the race and the winner
will be the one who followed through
Woman and Man
Stand!
Even if you're the only one on this land
GET RIGHT
FIGHT FOR YOUR LIFE!

My Worst Enemy

I never knew my worst enemy was me
Hard-headed, self-centered, lack of discipline,
destroying everything I touch and see
I knew it all
Never thinking one day I could fall
I lived for the moment, not thinking about the next day
Improving myself yeah, okay
Yet, I soon found that what goes around comes around
Now I'm the clown
Dropout, child on the way, bills to pay
So I sold, robbed, and stole
A brother almost got killed
Streets, survival of the fittest and who you know
Yet, keeping it real, some people don't want to see you grow
My peeps stabbed me in the back
Twenty-five years, man this mess is wack!
If only I knew my worst enemy was me
This world of hell I wouldn't have allowed myself to see
Caged up like a dog, treated and talked to like a child
Feelings of guilt drive me wild
I smile, for I remember when my mother, father,
family, loved ones, and counselors tried to warn me
Back then, when I was your age, I wasn't trying to see
Their points of view now if only I could choose
I would destroy that enemy that once lied within
I would deny that fast life filled with sin
I would take the road only traveled by few
My life is over, if only I knew

My young soldiers of today
you can choose to feel or block these words that flow your way
Yet, understand that when you play in hell's land
Your consequences I pray you can withstand
For, I was respected, loved amongst the streets
Fattest cars and tightest women that you would die to meet
As fast as it came, as fast as it went
This is why this message has been sent
Man, wake up, look around, and tell me what you see
Have you discovered that the enemy wasn't you, it was me!
SATAN!

Baby Steps

I want to break free

Yet,

It's hard to defeat the enemy

When the enemy is Me!

My past, my habits, and my daily routines

Block me from reality and accomplishing my dreams

Days turn into months and months turn into years

No change

No success brings on the spirit of fear!

Is This What I Have To Expect?

Living check by check

Countless men in and out of my life

Searching and praying for Mr. Right!

Bills stack like hills

Slowly watching my weight rise

Walking around with a smile, while on the inside I cry!

Voices telling me to grow up

Like cemented feet I try to move yet I'm stuck!

I want to release the strong woman that lies within

Yet,

My baggage is deep, where shall I begin?

Deny that which holds me back

You say

It isn't easy, it takes courage to survive each day

THE LORD SPEAKS,

My Child

You know where to begin

Open your heart and let me in!

You must deny sin or your life in darkness will never end
FATHER,
In other words, I must deny me
How can you be so faithful when I constantly defy thee?
Guilt,
Consciously surrounding myself by filth
Tilts my head down
How can I walk proudly calling myself a queen?
With a broken soiled crown on my head?
Finding comfort in pity instead of good
If Only I Could?
What is the true problem?
I'm lazy, disorganized, and a procrastinator
What is the true problem?
I don't appreciate my blessings, I put myself
down, and I'm my worst hater
What is the true problem?
I don't unconditionally love myself
I base my self-worth on the opinions of someone else
Now, we're peeling through
My Child
You will never be happy until you accept you for you
Accept your mistakes, understand them,
and move on throughout your test!
BABY STEPS
Are needed to achieve
Your Best!

G r o w !

Get it together
Row through the punches until we unite forever
Open your heart, sight what you see
We don't have that much time believe me!

STOP FEELING SORRY FOR YOURSELF
Whoever told you that the road would be easy?
Know, some of that pain you brought upon yourself
Trying to please and be somebody else!
You're drunk,
Drunk on fortune and fame
Got every scheme to build up your own name
Couldn't you understand?
That until you do God's will on this land
Hell will pour
Don't you know that you can't fill that
void, you will always seek more!
And watch where you return
You will always repeat the same cycle until you learn
How to surrender
How to let go
Don't you dare pass off this message for you should know!
It's I Am That I Am
Creator and Ruler over this land
I will have my way
You see,
In spite of what you're going through
I made you for this new day

Heed what I say!

Many will come in My Name

Telling you what is rightfully for you to claim

And It's a shame

That many won't make it through

Because they kept feeling sorry for themselves, just like you!

You know what to do

Let it go!

My Child

In the Name of Jesus

GROW!

Get it together

Row through the punches until we unite forever

Open your heart, sight what you see

We don't have that much time believe me!

Smoke

Get High

One Day You'll Wish To Die!

NO LIE
I watched the effects of Cancer
But, still I smoked
I heard about all the toxic chemicals found
But, still I got down on the choke
Then all of a sudden murder she wrote
I couldn't believe that high from that dope
That drug made a brother place a rope around my neck
Slowly losing all the things that I had in check
Then
Murder she wrote once again met
Let me slow down and tell
The Devil is already defeated. He can't kill you, but
he can influence you to die for the glory of hell!
Watch your friends
So many of them know that they are not going
anywhere so they try to pull you down before
your dream even has a chance to begin
Sin
Ain't nothing to mess with
Yo, God is known for destroying
Watch the road you travel
Watch this new venture you want to take
Not well thought of plans can mess up your fate

So, I guess you're wondering why a brother

took this moment to speak

I guess it's kind of lonely living six feet deep beneath the ground

It was truly my last get down

You know I couldn't breathe

Man that's the worst feeling ever

Then it was like all my major organs gave out on me together

I though back to when I was in your same shoes

When It didn't affect me like this

When I had the opportunity to choose

Life or Death

I tell you that smoke is a sure threat to your one and

only body that you can't get back or replace

I'm dead. I rest my case.

Keep on doing what you're doing, and

you too will embrace death

No lie

SMOKE GET HIGH

ONE DAY YOU'LL WISH TO DIE, PAIN HURTS NO LIE

LIVE IS MY LAST CRY

BYE!

United We Stand United We Fall

THIS IS FOR ALL

While I was sleeping
The police plotted to lock up the majority of our youth
While I was distracted
The drugs in our community grew, I guess
I was too high to notice the truth
While I was chilling
Healthcare was being slowly taken away
While I was playing
More people were going hungry, more and more everyday
While I was having fun
More lives were being taken from the hands of a gun
While I was refusing to work
I never took the time to analyze that all my
procrastination would eventually hurt
While I was caught up, too busy worrying about who I can love
Aids and other deadly diseases were being created and spread
While I was, I rarely took the time to fully use my head
While I was lead
By negativity
I didn't take the time to break down our race's reality
We are a dying breed
So, few actually stand up to lead
Yet so many gave up on what they believe
I'll bet
Even now while I'm speaking
So many of you are still sleeping

Wake up!

Don't wait until it happens to you to get fed up

Face the truth

Before our race is permanently stuck in hell

Read this and tell all

UNITED WE STAND OR UNITED WE FALL!

Freedom of Choice

Comes with a great cost, please hear my voice!

I understand
That there are many reasons to abort your seed on this land
But, do know!
That even after the abortion that feeling of
loss, emptiness, and guilt will grow!
It hurts!
To take a life
Having that endless wrong that you could never make right!
I wish
But, it's too late
I wish that I had that opportunity again to change my fate!
And let life live for Goodness Sake!
No wonder what that seed could have been, now
I have to die with my greatest mistake!
I know there are circumstances, some that seem so far
beyond your means, but there are other options
Praise God for the barren woman where her only choice is adoption
Where she receives that life blessing
And if you already had an abortion please learn from this lesson
That if we confess our sin, God is able to forgive and make whole
You will still feel your loss, but God and your forgiveness to
others and you will help you find peace within your Soul
So, let it be told
Scripture says, that children are a heritage from
the Lord, offspring a reward from him.
Blessed is the man whose quiver is full of them (Psalm 127:3-5)

*God said, "Before I formed you in the womb I knew
you, before you were born, I set you apart; I appointed
you as a prophet to the nations." (Jeremiah 1:5)*
My Child, surrender and grow in patience
And accept this reality!
*For you created my inmost being; you knit me together
in my mother's womb. I praise you because I am fearfully
and wonderfully made; your works are wonderful; I know
that full well. My frame was not hidden from you when I
was made in the secret place, when I was woven together
in the depths of the Earth. Your eyes saw my unformed
body; all the days ordained for me were written in your
book before one of them came to be. (Psalm 139:13-16)*
GOD PLEASE FORGIVE ME!
AS I FORGIVE OTHERS
Let my wrong inspire others to CHOOSE Life
instead of Death My Sisters and Brothers
Yes,
There are some very extreme situations, but
if you have the choice to do right!
I shout!
Fight for Your Unborn Child's Life!
Fight for Your Own Sanity!
I told you before, trust me!

Freedom of Choice
Comes with a great cost, please hear my voice!

Suicide

The taking of one's own life, please pay
close attention to my cry!

For scripture says, that God is the giver of life.
He gives, and He takes away (Job 1:21)
Our times are in your hands (Psalm 31:15)
Suicide or self-murder rejects God's gift of life and
it takes God's authority for only He decides when
and how a person should die on this land
Yet, I understand
How life's heavy loads can bear you down
No peace, no rest, and no happiness to be found
Yet, receive this that I write
In this time of darkness, I just need you
to shout out, "JESUS CHRIST!"
For He said come to Me, ALL you who are weary and
burdened, and I will give you rest. Take My yoke upon
you and learn from Me, for I am gentle and humble in
heart, and you will find rest for your Souls. For my yoke
is easy and my burden is light (Matthew 11:28-30)
But, he who fails to find me injures himself; all who
hate me love death (Proverbs 8:36) this is true!
Do you not know that you are God's temple and that
God's Spirit dwells in you? (1 Corinthians 3:16)

For the thief comes only to steal and kill and destroy. I came
that they may have life and have it abundantly (John 10:10)
I'm shouting out to the world that God is the answer
to surpass any hardship, hate, and tragedy!

And if we confess our sins, He is faithful and just to forgive
us our sins and to cleanse us from all unrighteousness
for His anger lasts only a moment but His favor, a
lifetime. Weeping may endure for a night, but joy
cometh in the morning (1 John 1:9) (Psalm 30:5)
Yes, live to see another sunshine!
Be not overly wicked, neither be a fool. Why should
you die before your time? (Ecclesiastes 7:17)
And Hell is worse than living on Earth!
Live to see another day and walk into your worth!
So, let us put down those things that kill
And let the Word of God instill
Within you!
Now you're living in your breakthrough!
Trust in the Lord with all your heart and lean not to
your understanding in all your ways submit to Him and
He will make your paths straight (Proverbs 3:5-6)
You're right on time and not late!
For this is your Word sent to heal and
make what was empty whole
Forgiveness is the key, so let it be told
That you are loved by God
Don't let the evil one rob
Your one and only greatest gift
Life!
Tell your enemies, even the enemy that is
in you, that I will live and not die!
No more thoughts or attempts at

Suicide!

Lost By Love

This poem is my healing process
You see,
In order for me to grow
I must let go!
As a child I hungered for the absent love of my father
I can recall his broken promises as I sat waiting for his return
Only to learn one day that my father was dead
My thirst for male attention led me into a world of shame
I can't get upset, for at the day's end there
was nobody to blame but myself
My focus left me, and I dedicated my life to someone else
I searched and I searched for love until I lost me
Allowing countess men to enter my body
Eating away my purity, corrupting my soul
There's no wonder why I find it hard to become whole
I loved,
I mean I loved to the point that I placed myself last
Satisfying all his needs
Because I believed that our relationship would succeed
To a higher level, to the point of unconditional love
Yet,
Only that feeling can be truly manifested from above
As the seasons change man will sin
Like a rose love blossom. As it dies a
new interest begins to grow.
It's that curiosity that forces you to know
What he tastes like, will he please you right
Damn his game is tight, should I give him some tonight?

My infested wounds are deep
Those demons are hunting me to the
point that I can't hardly sleep
I allowed myself to be a victim
Exposing myself to the chance of pregnancies and STDs
On the real
There have been many nights that I fell down on my knees
In tears, pleading God for forgiveness and mercy
My endless hope to live right
I get focused but the devil tricks me by bringing
an even more tempting candidate into my life
Then the cycle continues again, twenty-
six and still not able to win
My fear of being alone enabled me to
be Lost by Love, to fall weak
I tell myself
I can't dwell on the past, I'm still alive I have time to seek
My inner voice that keeps telling me to be still
Only then will my infested wounds heal
It's not going to be easy, yet your rewards will be of abundance
THE LORD SPEAKS
It is I, my child that you must seek!
Where your soul dwells, this private
chamber must be held tight!
If not, Satan will steal your life!
Don't ignore the signs, you truly know when it's time to let go
To have faith in Me is to have faith in you
Cleanse
Believe
Then your soul mate will be granted to you

LORD, my way has hardened my heart, has
turned me against love, against marriage
My child
I will ease your baggage
You Are No Longer Lost by Love
Yet,
Love Is Lost by You
For,
You remained faithful and your heart is true
MY EVE
You Must Believe
In YOU!

Sister Girlfriend

If that man wants to leave, let him!

For where you're going

God's Glory is straight showing

He can't handle that

Now here's another fact

Virtuous Lady

You tried

Where others would have doubted, you survived

And grew stronger through the process

Don't you dare feel less

But know that God knows what is best

So be still

Take this brief moment to heal

To instill what you so desire

Just know that with each test you grew higher

To the Lord

Sister Girlfriend, God is only pulling you more!

Don't you see?

That what is coming is beyond your Earthly reality

Where purpose immerses with destiny

To be one

This is your season; this is your time for the truth has come

Shake off that dirt

Release all that unnecessary hurt

Sister Girlfriend, walk into your worth!

It ain't easy

No one said that the road was easy

But you will make it through

It's just time to do right by you!

So let others leave

Pick up your broken pieces and recreate your dreams

Believe

That your red carpet awaits

God will set a table for you in front of all those that hate

It's time to celebrate a new beginning of the end!

It's all about you

SISTER GIRLFRIEND!

Be
Still!

BE STILL

Allow yourself time to heal

Time to fall in love with you

Time to accomplish all the goals that you said you wanted to!

BE STILL

For, fast living will kill!

Corrupting your soul

Trying to fill your emptiness while it is Me

that can only make you whole!

BE STILL

I shall build

Your promised land

Give me your hand

I shall help you understand

Your purpose, your reason for life!

BE STILL

Allow me to lead you right!

I Am

Your

Shining Light!

I pray these words you feel

For,
Our FATHER
Is telling us
MY
BROTHERS and SISTERS

TO
BE STILL!

Chapter 5
BUT GOD!

"For the Lord your God is the one who goes with you to fight for you against your enemies to give you victory." (Deuteronomy 20:4 NIV)

"So be strong and courageous! Do not be afraid and do not panic before them. For the Lord your God will personally go ahead of you. He will neither fail you nor abandon you." (NLT)

"He said, "If now I have favor in Your sight, O Lord, I pray, let the Lord go along in our midst, even though the people are so obstinate, and pardon our iniquity and our sin, and take us as Your own possession." (Exodus 34:9 NASV)

But GOD!

Listen to these words and don't allow the enemy to rob!

Holy Spirit come upon me as I speak and write
Lead me to deliver a Word that will transform lives
For, this is the day that the Lord has made we will
rejoice and be glad in it! (Psalm 118:24)
Pay close attention for this was meant!

In the beginning, God created man in His own likeness
and image that He may fulfill the Word of God
But the enemy
Came up to steal, kill, and destroy what God
has planned for both you and me
So, do know, My Child, that when fighting the enemy
You have to use the Word of God to claim victory
So, repeat these words that I speak daily
And have faith that God hears me

I should have died!
But God is my refuge and strength, a very
present help in trouble (Psalm 46:1)
Lead
Me safely through
Though I walk in the midst of trouble, you preserve my life;
you stretch out your hand against the wrath of my enemies,
and your right hand delivers me too (Psalm 138:7)
I'm shouting out to the world that *Every*
Word of God proves true! (Psalm 16:8)

I lived a life surrounded by sin
But God is a shield to those who take refuge in him (Psalm 16:8)
He himself bore our sins in His body on the cross so
that we might die to sins and live for righteousness; by
His wounds you have been healed (1 Peter 2:24)
I tell you that the evil one tried his best to hinder and kill!
I had so much hate, negative people trying to
destroy my fate, preying on my downfalls
Scripture says that many are the afflictions of the righteous,
but God delivers him or her out of them all! (Psalm 34:19)
I confess, Lord, please hear me
For scripture says, that whoever conceals their sins
does not prosper, but the one who confesses and
renounces them finds mercy (Proverbs 28:13)
I made so many wrong choices
Denying and ignoring the wisdom sent
through your inner voices
I panicked, I stressed out, Lord did I shout!
I moved without thinking and failed to follow through
But God, is my keeper my shade on my right hand
God himself watches over you (Psalm 121)
I kept speaking the Word of God through
it all and believed for sure
That the Lord will watch over your coming
and going both now and forevermore
Even when love left
By choice or by death
God gave me a peace that surpasses all understanding, and He
guarded my heart and my mind in Christ Jesus (Philippians 4:7)
I'm telling you only in God do we place our trust

For if God is for us who or what can be against us (Romans 8:31)
Plus, scripture says, that the Lord is close to the
brokenhearted; he rescues those whose spirits are crushed
I will not die; instead I will live to tell what the Lord has done
How He healed my body and redeemed me from certain
death and met my needs, each and every one
It is finished it is done! *(John 19:30)*
For I can do all things through Christ who
gives me strength (Philippians 4:13)
Hallelujah Lord, I shout out your highest thanks!
You are my God, and I will praise you!
You are my God, and I will exalt you! (Psalm 118:28)
For, the stone that the builders rejected has now become the
cornerstone and this is the Lord's doing too (Psalm 118:22)
I shout out, give thanks to the Lord for he is good and
his faithful love endures forever! (Psalm 29)
Never! Give Up!
For the devil is a liar
He will use him and her
To deceive
To make you not believe
That what you speak with faith and works shall be fulfilled
If you desire to heal, to instill, and to
kill the old to be a better you
Then, receive my final truth
No matter what the evil one and his armies
try to plan to steal, to kill, and to rob!
There is already a solution, grace, salvation,
or an escape route just trust and speak
BUT GOD!
Katrina T. Smith

My King

My Liberty Bell that forever rings
I'm declaring my love to You
My Good Shepherd, My Prince of Peace,
My One who's always True
No one or nothing is greater than thee
My Lord and Savior, I fall bent on one knee
Surely knowing that Your Victory has been bestowed upon me
You see,
You are My Provider
My Fruits of the Spirit Supplier
You are My Prosperity
Greater than riches you are to me
My Holy Trinity
You fill me
Protect me from my enemies, even the enemy that lives in me
You are My Lover
Good loving all day, all night, to that
revealed to even under the cover
I feel a feeling that I never felt before
You see only with You do I reach and become more
I praise you every day of my life, even after my death
I praise you Jesus for you have paid all our debts
Took in and overcame all our threats
May these words, "Glory Father, Glory unto You"
Forever flow through to You
I sing
That I will forever wear Your Wedding Ring!
I sing unfailing praises and kisses of love to YOU My Forever
MY KING

Thank You GOD for Your Power!

Thank You The Great "I AM" That "I
AM" for this life-changing hour!
For I Feel Your Grace
The Word said that the first shall be last
and the last shall be first in this race
Thank You Lord for this taste
Of Your Greatness, may our Father be given all the Glory
For supernaturally changing my life-story
Savior Jesus Christ, I pray
May
You walk with me through it all
From success to even my downfall
For I can't move without You
Abba my Daddy please guide your baby through
You have all of me!
Praises be unto God who allows the blind to see
The deaf to hear
The victory even over fear
May my Spirit intertwine with Your Spirit as one
Holy Trinity hallelujah, the Truth has come
I confess this is the hour!
To
Thank You GOD for Your Power!
In Jesus' Matchless Name
Amen!
LET THE WORKS OF OUR FATHERGODSPIRIT BEGIN!
AMEN!

You Were Born to WIN!

So, know that victory belongs to JESUS who
holds the keys of life and death by sin
Pay close attention and let God in!
My age I cannot speak
But child, I've been around here long enough
to know what keeps you weak
Yes, child I have the answer to the question you seek
Why?
Why this test?
To see where your soul shall forever rest
Heaven or Hell
In due time the answer to that question our Lord will tell
But you must think deeper than what you daily see
This is a generational thing, our ancestors
living through both you and me
What's my purpose you ask?
Well, here is a fact
To serve, to praise God
For keeping you another day despite what
you allowed the enemy to rob
Our job is to worship You
Our only one God who is so holy, merciful, and always true
Go ahead and admit Abba, my Father, my Daddy I need you!
To help me while I pass through
This test
That despite it all you give me peace of mind and rest
I confess,
All my sins and weaknesses of the flesh

Help me to live out my best
Life
Help me Lord live right!
The Lord Speaks
My Son and My Daughter
Today I give to you My Living Water
Greater works than I have done you shall do
The Great I AM That I AM is the Creator, so
hold tight His Words are only True

Thanksgiving

Is a time to give thanks!

To thank God for keeping your mind sane, your

soul whole, and your body in strength

To thank your family for their unfailing love

To be thankful for all the trials and

tribulations that you rose above

Thanksgiving is a time to share

Your appreciation to all those you hold so dear

To show them that you truly care

Let us take this moment to pause

For this time in history cause

For a deeper touch

Let us thank our FatherGodSpirit for allowing each of us

To experience each other another year

For so many have lost loved ones throughout the years

Right now, their tears

Are not of joy but pain

Let us claim

Our victory

Let us live out our lives for the glory of our Almighty

God

Let us speak by faith that we will receive a

hundred-fold of what the devil tried to rob

Our joy, our finances, our health, our life

Let this prayer lend us into right

For one day

Our souls on this Earth shall be no more

One day we pray to be in the home of the Lord

So let us say

I love you to all as we share our meal together today

For this is true

With all that I am and shall become, forever more I love you

Thanks for Giving

Amen

Only through Jesus Christ do we have victory over sin

God is Greater!

So, don't fear bad weather, news, and the taunts of your haters
You show God's love by forgiving and
unfailingly loving all your neighbors
Do!
And it shall be given unto you
For you are blessed and highly favored by God
All these things shall be giving a billion-
fold of what was robbed
For, Greater is God than he or it of this world
Use your talents to uplift all men, women, boys, and girls
For the time has come
My Dear Chosen One
To spread your wings and fly
Flying high amongst the sky
For your dreams are bigger than you can do yourself
So, learn to depend on and to submit to someone else
For, the greatest good
Use your gifts to uplift and pull others
out of the ghetto and hood
I wish I could touch you and hold you tight
For, this is a fight for your soul's life
Get Right
And get dressed for church to go hear the Word!
Trust, eventually you live out what is heard
For no man can stop what God has
already ordained as His own
I pray, let His Holy Spirit live in your
body, your temple, your home

I promise with God you're never alone
I speak victory
I hope you hear me
Greatness, Purity, Holiness, and Wholeness
For you are greater than this!
I speak, rise up, him and her!
Pick up your bed, walk into your true
worth, and sin no more for

God is Greater!

Lord, Help Me!

Help me bring out all that lies in me right now in my reality
Help Me!
From myself
Help me with all these businesses and ministries
that were meant to uplift someone else
Help me eat better and take care of my health
Help me live with financial overflow. Lord
bless my Soul and my wealth.
Lord, help me with my dream home
Lord, cover me, keep me, never leave me alone
Lord, help me not compare to others
Help me unfailingly love all my sisters and brothers
Help me with my husband or wife so I can no
longer waste my time with unworthy lovers
Lord, help me with my self-esteem
FatherGodSpirit help me accomplish all my dreams
Lord, help me make our Father's Will on Earth come true
Lord, help me kill those things that block my breakthrough
Lord, I need You
Now!
Lord, help me with those things inside
of me that have not been found
Help me live with my crown
For I AM a Child of God
Father, replenish all that which that has been robbed
Lord, increase my income on my job
Help me appreciate and not to hate
Help me forgive so that I may live

Lord, I pour out all my fears, worries, and self-doubts

Please answer my prayers, I shout!

For, I need you like I need air to breathe

Lord, lead

My way

Help me make the most out of each day

Guard what I say

Lord, touch all and me

Lord, help me be happy

In the midst of the storm

Lord, I pray to help me be strong

Give me a new mind, create in me a clean heart

Lord, help me with this new start

Because it's time to live in my true destiny!

I pray

Lord, Help Me!

Abba! My Daddy

How Great thou are
Our Brightest Star
Your Glory covers us both near and far
I just can't stop repeating "How Great thou are!"
You know what is good for me and against
You are the greatest Daddy, daily I see your
blessings. I shout, "I got evidence!"
Of how Great thou are to me
I mean, I have no life without the Holy Trinity
In the Name of the Father, Son, and Holy Spirit
Lord, I praise you all day long and I pray that you hear it
For, You are Worthy all Glory be given unto You
Our Beginning and Our End, Our Forever True
I don't just love but I AM without question in love with You!
You made and make me who I AM, willingly I serve
For, in all goodness unfailing praise you deserve
You are the ultimate Superstar!

ABBA My DADDY
How Great Thou Are!

Defiling the Temple

Making your body a living sacrifice
Surely comes with a price
I mean you have to completely change your life
Where in all things you keep God in sight
This is why I write
Why I share
Because God cares about what you put in your
body, our holy temple where Christ dwells
Stop giving glory to hell
By partaking in those forbidden pleasures
And measure the weight
How those bad habits just take
Your presence on this Earth is needed; what
God placed in you can change a world
Giving hope and unfailing love to all
men, women, boys, and girls
The answer is simple!

Stop Defiling Your Temple!

GOD is Magnificent!

Yahweh

Have it Your Way

Our Lord

Of more

How magnificent is Your Name

I unfailingly claim

Throughout the Earth

Today I walked into my true worth!

Yes,

Through Jesus Immanuel our Christ

Today we honor your sacrifice

The laying down of your life

So, we can rejoice and boost in the Great I

AM That I AM Creator of All Things

Our love, our breath, our everything

We sing

Praises of our many victories

Of how God conquered all our enemies,

even the enemy that lives in me

Glory to your Holy Unfailing Sovereign and all-knowing Name

A Name above all names

In You our minds, bodies, and souls forever remain

Your Children just wanted our Abba, our Daddy, to know

That we thank you and appreciate you even

in death, to every day we grow

Closer to You

Our final destination, our Breakthrough

For to be in Your Presence is Priceless;
truly it is the greatest honor of man
To stand
Before our FatherGodSpirit our Beginning and our End
Our Savior from all sin
Yes, You
Who thought this was meant for others
but came straight to You!
God wants to use You for His Glory
Trust, all your trials and tribulations were just a
testimony of His Good Works in Your Life Story
Praise Him, focus on the Good News, and
speak this Word constantly!
Speak GOD is Magnificent!
Yahweh
Have it Your Way
Our Lord of more
How magnificent is Your Name!
I unfailingly claim
Throughout the Earth
Today I walked into my true worth!

My Husband

In Whom I Unfailingly TRUST
IMMANUEL GOD WITH US
My Beginning and My End
My Forever Lover, Partner, Protector, and Best Friend
So, let it be written, so know this to be true
With all my mind, body, and soul, My GOD I Love You!
The Holy Trinity
Three and One FatherGodSpirit I surrendered
because you first chose me
To be your Eternal Bride for eternity
I pray,
That it happens endlessly, whatever brings
joy, happiness, and Glory Your Way
For, You are Worthy to be praised
Savior, I thank you for giving me victory and
shielding me in these trialing days
For strengthening my mind, body, and
soul, and for steadying my way
You are to me My Air that I need to breathe in order to live
You are to me My Sun that I need for Life,
just like the Sun you unfailingly give
You are my Boo, my Road Dog, my Best Man
I declare to the World that only in and through you do I stand
Obtaining blessings coming in and going out all over this land
Today, I found my greatest gift, my purpose for
life, and the reason to why I AM here
To SHARE your unfailing love, grace,
mercy, healing, and saving power

To tell all that this is the hour

To declare your love unto God

To focus on the good and not on the enemy's tactics that rob

Your joy, your peace,

That kills you from the inside out until you speak defeat

My Husband

Stood to His Feet

And Made our Father's Will Come True

Jesus Died for both me and you

So that we may have life and have life more abundantly

Please don't ignore me

For the time has come

Ready or Not

Victory belongs to JESUS, so we've already WON!

Come out!

I Shout!

For We Were Born to WIN!

I tell you that there is no Greater Love

than the Heavenly Love of

My Husband

In Whom I Unfailingly TRUST

IMMANUEL GOD WITH US

I Smile

Because God is my Beginning and my End
He only knows what, how, and when
In my life
I Smile because Jesus is my Christ
No weapon formed against me shall prosper for
Greater is He that is in me than he of this world
This message is for you, my man, woman, boy, and girl
Through the tears, smile
Through your greatest nightmares and fears, smile
For Victory already belongs to Jesus, therefore,
Victory already belongs to You
You are a Child of God, stay true
Love the Lord with all your mind, with all your body, and with
all your soul, and love your neighbors as you love yourself
That there is the problem
Too many people are not loving themselves
And how do you bring about self-love?
First, you surrender yourself to the Great I AM That I AM our
Heavenly Father who dwells from below, between, and above
Then you FLUSH
Forgive yourself and others, Let it go, Understand we are
all human and we all make mistakes, Share your learnings,
and be Harmonious, humble yourself and be a peacemaker
Realize that you grow from your haters
So, SMILE
And Focus on the Good
And no more, "I wish I could."
Because now you can

I AM is telling you that you were born to win!

Come as you are

From the lowly to a superstar

All are welcomed to enjoy in the rest of life, in the peace

With God, all things are possible, obtaining

victory in a once thought easy defeat

Our God stood to His feet

And His Strong Right Arm protected and shielded me

For this moment I was born and my assignment

willingly I accepted from the Holy Trinity

To tell you to trust God, for when you need

an answer just give him a dial!

And remember the battle is already won,

so don't worry just trust God and

SMILE!

Shine in the darkness

Make God your only source

In yourself always believe and

Love

Everyone

SMILE!

Lord, I Thank You for Another Blessed Day!

For sending your favor, grace, and mercy my way
Please heed to what I say
My Abba, My Daddy who forever dwells
Who has all keys over Heaven and Hell
May I tell
You thanks!
For keeping me in Your unfailing strength
For being with me every moment, every
second, and every breath
Lord, I praise you for overcoming all my threats
NO ONE IS GREATER THAN THE GREAT
I AM THAT I AM RULER OVER ALL
God even lets victory come from my downfalls
For, His strength, His power is made perfect in my weakness
And I forgave
I focused on the good and even in the storm in God I praised
For, I am blessed coming in and going out
"Victory belongs to Jesus our Christ," I shout!
And the evening time just gets better
I tell you don't stress, just relax and trust
that God protects from all weather
And high water
I know that you thought this was for someone else, but
I AM is talking to you, my dear son and daughter
Be grateful, give thanks, and heed to what I say

Supernatural, unexplainable, and sudden
abundancy is coming your way!
From this day forward all you can believe, speak it, and say,
"Even through the storm
Lord, I Thank You for Another Blessed Day!"

I'm Coming Out!

"Victory is mine through Christ Jesus
our Lord and Savior," I shout!
No more living in fear, laziness, confusion, hurt, and self-doubt!
Every day
Forward I commission the Holy Trinity to lead my way
To direct what I do and say
For, God so loved the world that He gave
His one and only begotten Son
Yet, it was part of the process so that our union back in
Paradise in Heaven in His Holy Garden of Eden may come
For what the devil meant for evil will come to the Glory of God!
Endless blessings stored in the Kingdom of
God have opened unto us for all which was
inherited, held back, deferred, and robbed!
For Greater is God that lives in me than
he or it that lives in the world
I'm coming out for you, my dear man, woman, boy, and girl
God's thoughts and ways are far above my thoughts and ways
So, I can't tell you how, but surely as the Word says
Jesus came that I may have life and have it more abundantly
Both Here on Earth and in Heaven I shall
have victory for all eternity!
For, God chose me
Even before I knew myself
On the real, just as cancer kills
I am telling you that you can't win this
race without God Himself!

What a joy and peace you shall feel as
you feast amongst your enemies
Conquering even the enemy that lives in me
This is a first,
But to stop that vicious curse
You have to search deep within
Over your own mindset you must win
But it starts with confessing, then forgiving, then
on to winning, by loving others and yourself
It is a sacrifice, but it is well worth it to drop
that negative habit and be your better self
So, one day you too can shout!
In the Name of Jesus, I'm Out!
"Make God your Lord and Savior Today," I Shout!
Just speak, with you Lord only AM I Out
Then go find a church home and grow
Let the Lord use you as only He knows!

CHILD of GOD GO!

Sacrifices of Thanks!

FatherGodSpirit

I thank you for keeping me and for making

all my weaknesses your Strengths

For your power is made perfect in my weakness

And deepest

Fears

I thank you for providing for all my needs, wants, and cares

I thank you for protecting me through the storm

Sheltered by your strong right arm

There is no me with you

Lord of Heaven's armies, I pray every day to let

our Father's will for my life come true

Wow,

I thank you for keeping me from death

Daddy, you stepped in and overcame all threats

It's like onto the next

Yes,

I do confess

That we are meant to build thou Kingdom Come here on Earth

I thank you Jesus for because of your self-

sacrifice I can walk in my true worth

I thank you in advance for all that you have prepared for me

All good things come from the Great I AM that I AM Almighty

All traps have been broken and my Child you are set free

To fly like an eagle and live life even more abundantly

For I confess

No matter rich or poor, healthy or sick, victorious or lost,

God has always kept me highly favored and blessed!

And filled with a joy that no one can steal
I pray that even my mistakes prosper in
Jesus' Matchless Name, amen for real
I can't do this by myself
And the Lord is teaching me to humble myself
To care for others and be your better self
You know,
The person inside of you longing to come out
Well, now is that transition to no longer
live in fear and self-doubt
For greater is He that is in you than he
or it that is of this world I shout
Trust,
Rest in peace and surely know that the Lord
already made a way out for us
There are some things that we can't control
God truly knows when it's our time to shine for
His Glory; Daddy let the truth unfold
For had it not been for the Lord on my side
where, O Lord, where would I be?
For I had so many enemies
Daily trying to bind me
Most importantly the enemy that lived in me
Whispering negative thoughts and
keeping me off track and so busy
But God!
God returned an unlimited flow of what the enemy robbed
Like Job
He stored his fortunes when Job prayed for his friends
This is the way of our Beginning and our End

God loves yet he hates sin
He hates it so much that he gave his one and only Son,
Jesus Christ, to die so that our new life in him may begin
Therefore, all who confess Jesus as their Lord
Shall inherit Heaven, Paradise, and
live in good health and more
More joy, more peace, before your enemies you will feast
Lord, I can continue repeatedly all day and night long
to praise you for your unfailing love, tender-kindness,
mercy, grace, protection, power, and unfailing strength!
My only God and forever Love receive eternally my continuous

Sacrifices of Thanks!

This is Dedicated to My Smokers, To My All Day and Night Chokers!

Throw It Away!
Don't you dare go buy another pack or
make a transaction today!
Smoking has 7,000 chemicals with 70 of them deadly to you
Today, I rebuke the devil, that enemy no
longer lives, today you breakthrough
And use your common sense
Don't fake, this was meant
You are greater!
You are worth more than stressing and smoking over your
enemies, family, friends, loved ones, and neighbors
You need to live and love life!
People want to see you prosper, choose right!
Because smoking kills!
I'm living because Jesus Christ died for my sins and that Word
I speak and act in for our God Who Art in Heaven is Real!
Surrender today
And say,
"FatherGodSpirit, the Holy Trinity,
Erase the thought of me smoking, the first day
that I picked it up, from my memory.
I thank you in advance for taking away the
taste, the cravings, the routines,
And Lord I pray not in my strength, yet in
Your Holy Spirit, keep me clean
For the devil is a liar

I will not die

To this weakness

For God's power is made perfect in my weakness.

Therefore, victory is mine."

If you're reading this, I promise that

you will put it down this time

Because no more denial

No more child

The adult in me, I brought the courage to believe

That I will be healthy and teach others to succeed

For I accept Jesus as my Christ

Only through Him do I obtain the Father,

the Great I AM that I AM

While I was reading, He was changing me to forever stand

In His Greatness I live on this land

I speak in faith today!

In Jesus' Matchless Name No Consequences to

my Body, my Spirit, and my Mind I Say!

This is my sign

Throw It Away!

Today!

And fill that gap immediately with positive

things; heed to what I Say

Throw It ALL ALWAY!

I Praise You!

Hallelujah to our God who is so holy and so true
FatherGodSpirit
I love you, with every being of my soul
Daddy fill me with your Living Water that I might be whole
Through the Blood of Jesus, I claim victory
The Word of God leads me
My Husband, my Wife
For eternity about your Goodness, I could write
For your Spirit, I can feel
All over my body, I shout to the world that God is real!
My joy, my patience, my peace
My victor even in my defeat
I pour out, I surrender all for just a touch
For if God is for us, who or what can be against us?
Only in You, FatherGodSpirit I trust
Let all that I am and shall be
From the top of my head to the bottom of my body I praise thee
My Creator, my Master, my Lover, my Forever Best Friend
My Beginning and my End
Come in
Like a flood
Fill me with your unfailing mercy, grace, joy,
kindness, tenderness, faithfulness, and love
With my last breath and thought my
King, receive this which is true
With all my heart, mind, body, and soul I will still
Praise YOU!
Only you can quench my thirst

For you loved me first!
So much that you gave your life so that I may live
While I am here in the land of the living, Lord use me to give!
Come through!
Hallelujah
FatherGodSpirit

I Praise You!

GOD

Turned It All Around in My Favor!

He gave me victory over all my enemies while

sharing with me His Goodness, Loving-Kindness,

Mercy, and Grace through all my neighbors!

He opened closed doors

When they took, Jesus blessed me with more

God made a way out of no way

My Daddy guards and keeps me through

the night to each new day

He went before me so what is needed

has already been provided for

For sure,

You have confidence because you trust

whole-heartedly in our Lord!

Jesus is my Husband, my Lover, My Good-

Counselor, My Forever Best Friend

I Am a Child of the Great I AM that I

AM, our Beginning and our End

We come boldly before God because Jesus died for all our sin!

We now have through Christ a new beginning!

And easier than what it seems

Don't hate, for we are living in our true dream!

What was bounded is now released

What used to kill has now ceased

Our Father Chose you for a reason

In this season

His purpose will be made clear

Fear not

It all will drop in your favor

You see, dear neighbor!

All year you will speak that

GOD

Turned It All Around in My Favor!

Chapter 6
MY CHOSEN ONE

"For many are called, but few are chosen." (Matthew 22:14 ESV)

"Furthermore, because we are united with Christ, we have received an inheritance from God, for he chose us in advance, and he makes everything work out according to his plan." (Ephesians 1:11 ESV)

"You did not choose me, but I chose you and appointed you that you should go and bear fruit and that your fruit should abide, so that whatever you ask the Father in my name, he may give it to you." (John 15:16 ESV)

An Oath
of
A Woman!

♦♦_____♦♦_____♦♦

You may put me down
But I am a queen, and I shall wear my crown!
You may say that I will never go anywhere
But this strong woman is making her way up the stairs!
You may try to hold me back
But don't think that you will ever have a chance to relax!
You may call me names
But I don't play into those games!
You may not like the color of my face
But I am proud of my background in race!
I am a woman who will not be stopped
Because my life goals are only at the top!
I am full of love
Which I inherited from above!
I was put on this Earth to bring
A strong unity of dreams!
That will come true for both me and you!
"Watch out," I shout!
Because it's time to claim
The Respect and Meaning
Of
A WOMAN'S NAME!

Black And Beautiful

I AM
Strength soars through
For the teachings of the Lord have just
begun for both me and you

BLACK AND BEAUTIFUL I AM
Carrying the burdens of my family
The burdens of my man, keeping them healthy and sound
A deep-rooted, strong foundation, instilled within the ground

BLACK AND BEAUTIFUL I KNOW
That an urgent need for sister and brotherhood must grow!
Why criticize when one can create?
An increase in love, self-esteem, respect
And a decrease in jealousy, phoniness, and hate

BLACK AND BEAUTIFUL I AM ONLY ONE
For, this takes the work of many to get the job done
"How can this be accomplished?" you say.
Send positives to those that you pass, each and every day
Then kindness shall be passed!

BLACK AND BLACK
BLACK AND BEAUTIFUL
MY BROTHERS AND SISTERS, WE
SHALL FOREVER LAST!

For a Fact,
I'm Proud to Be Black!

From our colorful skin
To our inner strength to fight
for our civil rights
I tell you that we were born to win
From the curl of our hips
To the beauty of our full lips
We have and still are shaping the foundation
of this nation
We are the innovators
Entrepreneurs that labor to uplift our neighbors
We are talent made perfect
I'm speaking straight to you my sisters and brothers,
strive for excellence for we are worth it
Every day that you live, I cry
Realize, that you are the new difference that this world seeks
From the blood of our ancestors there is no such thing as weak
Dear Black Woman and Black Man
Stand
Let us continue to stand for the truth
I tell you like our history movements formed from the youth
My final word
Let your voice be heard
Let your light so shine
For, now is our time
To finish what was started years ago
I shout knowledge we must know

Love, understanding, and forgiveness we must show

For greater are the things to come

I know you can hear me, my chosen one

Like the sunrise, even with tears in our eyes, we rise

Even as our young soldiers die

For the cause

I was sent here to tell you all

That Victory dwells in thee for a fact!

What color can overpower I Am Proud to be Black!

I Am Black History

The genes and blood of my ancestors' flow through me!
I AM unstoppable, I AM the seed of the free!
For through their pains, their breakthrough gains
I now claim
Victory!
I AM who I AM because of my past
I AM Black History!
Born to rule and conquer turning my
dreams into my daily reality
I AM hurt!
From the killings of our ancestors to the killings of each other
No respect for life murdering daily our sisters and brothers
before their dreams could manifest before returned to dirt!
I AM alert!
For the enemy only comes but to kill, steal, and
destroy what was destined to be birth!
Yet, no weapon formed against me shall prosper
So, I don't fear him or her
I move despite my flaws
I move for a new cause
Called I AM BLACK HISTORY!
Not a month but daily
I celebrate my culture, my roots, the
accomplishments of Black people near me
For as the sunrise
I AM BLACK HISTORY I will cry
Until oneness is met
The treasures of our ancestors must be kept

Let us move to our new groove

For it's no longer his story

But all the glory

Be given unto Me

I'M REAPING THE BLESSINGS OF MY ANCESTORS

WHILE STILL IN STORING OUR LEGACIES

THERE IS NO STOPPING ME!

FOR, FROM THE GENES AND BLOOD

OF OUR ANCESTORS

I TOLD YOU BEFORE THAT I AM

BLACK HISTORY!

Katrina T. Smith

WHEN THEY HIT LOW WE HIT HIGHER!

I NEED YOU TO PAY CLOSE ATTENTION FOR WE ARE DOWN TO THE WIRE!

So let it be said!

JESUS CHRIST told us to love your enemies because he

knew that it was a weapon to bruise Satan's heel and head

So don't be so easily mislead

When the enemies arrive

OUR LORD told us to pray for those who

persecute you, backstab, and lie

Because we are the true children of our Father in Heaven

made to be perfect even as our Father is perfect!

So, we understand that the victory belongs to

Jesus, so there is no need to have a fit!

OUR SAVIOR told us to bless those who curse you

Please understand that at the day's end this will

determine your Soul's breakthrough

OUR KING of Kings told us to do good to those who hate you

OUR PRINCE OF PEACE told us to

pray for those who mistreat you

In fact, be happy and glad about it, for a great reward

awaits you in Heaven and remember that our ancient

prophets were persecuted in the same way too

This is not a mistake; this message was meant straight for you!

Do to others whatever you would like

them to do to you and stay true!

For, the highway to hell is broad and its gate is
wide for the many who choose that way
But the gateway
To life is very narrow and the road is
difficult and only a few ever find it
I told you before to pay close attention
for this message was meant!
IT'S SEPARATION TIME!
AND OUR SOULS ARE WORTH MORE THAN
MATERIALISTIC THINGS, HATE, WAR,
VENGEANCE, VIOLENCE, ANGER, AND CRIME
FINAL RHYME
MY CHILDREN Satan comes to kill, steal,
and destroy; he is an accuser and a liar!
Children of God, take the narrow road and LOVE even

WHEN THEY HIT LOW,
WE HIT HIGHER!

When All Hell Pours In

That means the blessings are about to begin
And Satan can't stand to see you win

So, he makes you change your speech
He constantly wants you to speak which is weak
Over your life
He makes you feel guilty and want to hide out of sight
From Jesus our Lord, our Christ

He makes you worry about the responsibilities of life
Bills, food, clothing, your needs and your wants
So, you hunt
That which means you no good
Got you speaking, I should have, and I could

But Child
Dear Child, this you must know!
WHEN ALL HELL POURS IN
WELCOME
THAT
OPPORTUNITY
TO GROW!

Let the Spirit of God Flow!
Amen,
Tell yourself right now that I was born to win!

One Tenth

Lord this message is meant
And I know that I'm not by myself
There have been many
That withheld their tithe for themselves
And we want to know
Why won't our finances grow?
Quoting from a Scripture verse
"You are cursed with a curse." (Mal. 3:8,9)
For God, we have robbed only You
By our own ignorance, selfishness, and distrust
Have we blocked our own breakthrough!
And the Lord speaks to both me and you
"Test me in this (the tithe)." says the Lord Almighty,
"And see if I will not throw open the floodgates of
Heaven and pour out so much blessing that you will
not have room enough for it." (Mal. 3:10, N.I.V.)
God is pleading with us to be faithful in our one-tenth
I told you before that this is meant
That this message has been sent
That before your bills, your desires,
That before your spouse
"Bring all the tithes into the storehouse, that
there may be food in My house." (Mal. 3:10)
Lord
I denounce,
My old way of thinking. I place my faith in You
I rebuke the thoughts
That kept me from my financial breakthrough

I had my own reasons
And then it became a normal routine
But I know greater is He for Christ Jesus is my King of kings
Forgiveness I plead, create in me a new heart
I now welcome my tithe to start
I accept your test
And I pray Lord that these words are meant!
For I Honor You, Lord, With My

One Tenth

What Would Jesus Do?

Take this time to listen as I speak to you
Before you act or speak
I repeat
Before you act or speak, question you
I repeat, before you act or speak, what would Jesus do?
Know that this battle is spiritual; it's beyond you
It's about souls
Where either Heaven or Hell will hold
So let it be told
That Greater is He that is in you than
he or it that is of this world
It's time to get saved man, woman, little boy, and girl
To fight temptation
The damnation of this nation
You must always seek
First the Kingdom of Heaven and its
righteousness to reach your peak. I speak
The truth
You know you can hear me; daily I speak to you
And I sit back and watch how you deny me, too
How can you forget that I died for you?
That I'm in love with you
Whatsoever if it's for our Father's will
you speak, it shall be Done
This message was meant just for you, my Chosen One
One day you will have to choose before it chooses for you
One day you're going to have to face your breakthrough
I want you to love yourself enough that you will choose right

I want you to live a long, prosperous life
But there is something that you must do
Daily you must die to you
Daily you must labor for God's Will to come true
Before you act, before you speak,
Child this is it, I loose your strongholds that made you weak
In the Name of Jesus, Mighty God, come through
You will win every time, I promise you!
If you question before you act, before you speak,

What Would Jesus Do?

Let Thou Will Be Done

Over my life

Let every move I make be pleasing in Your sight

For I am always in the right place at the right time

For my footsteps are ordered by the Lord

FatherGodSpirit

Only in You do I obtain more

I place my faith in Thee

For this is only the way

That I can fulfill

What I was purposed to be

Lord

Stand

Live

In and Through Me!

By faith

Along with works

I believe that it has already Happened

Surely it shall come!

If I Only Remember To

Let Thou Will Be Done

Why Did You Doubt Me?

I HEARD THE LORD SAY
That my precious child, I have carried you all the way
Throughout your storm
I have held you in my strong arm
Yet, you still doubt
That I won't bring you out
Bow down, fall on your face, and give me praise
Only then will I raise your feeble legs
Give me all
I promise you, my child, that you would not fall
My Savior,
I'm laying it all on the line
I will undoubtedly trust You this time
Father, direct my steps to what is next to
claim in your reverent name
My child, ye of little faith,
I heard you say before that you wanted more
Yet, you didn't labor to fulfill your dream
You found out that it's harder than what it seems
Just do it, don't hold back
Believe that it's not just a dream, yet a proven fact!
Father,
I've been through so much on this Earth
My child it's through these tests that you find your worth
Yet, Father
You turned my whole world around
It's hard to smile while underneath I'm hiding a frown
Tell me, my child, have I ever let you down?

Yes, you may not understand why you had
to transform your old into new
Yet, trust Me, my child, you will make it through
To see
What you were created for Victory!
My Master,
I have learned to give you thanks
For you see each time I overcome I feel my new strength
I see you at the end of my test
Yet, my child, you too must confess
I hear you talk, but don't forget that every day I see!
And I just can't understand

WHY DID YOU DOUBT ME?

It Is Finished!

Your soul shall be at rest
I told you before that there's life after death
IT IS FINISHED
All threats brought to you are now through
You have been loosed to do what I purpose you to
IT IS FINISHED
Your finances are now overflowing
The blessings you waited for are now unfolding
IT IS FINISHED
That once love has now been forbidden from your life
You will live Christlike
IT IS FINISHED
Your true love has come
To accept and build upon You, My Chosen One
IT IS FINISHED
Your body is made whole, long life you shall embrace
I told you before
That the blessings are given to those that finish the race
IT IS FINISHED
Your seeds shall inherit the land
And bring forth a change that will make man stand
IT IS FINISHED
Your mind is renewed by My every Will
Your strength and wisdom I shall build
IT IS FINISHED
Your emotions are balanced
Even in the storms, you shall have peace
I told you before your enemies I prepared you a great feast

IT IS FINISHED
I am the Alpha and the Omega
THE BEGINNING AND THE END
IT IS FINISHED
FOR YOU NOW HAVE ALL THE AUTHORITY OVER SIN
You Will Just Watch and See
What All I Have Spoken Become a Reality
My Word Never Returns Void from Jesus Your Almighty
IT IS FINISHED ONLY IF YOU TRUST IN ME!

It's Time
This Is Your Season!

The Turn of the Century Has Come!
Where those that praise the Name of
Jesus shall be united as one
Overflow of blessings has begun
Those that were looked over are now viewed as someone
My Child, you are growing
Your anointed gifts that were deferred are showing
Shining bright amongst this world
No more childish thinking, no more little boy and girl
You stand bolding in My Name
Even when against the rule you are willing to claim
You surrendered, you welcomed Me into your soul
You labored faithfully to maintain balance
And make what was empty whole
You know it too
Many are just starting to recognize
the real you coming through
Many days you prayed
Unto Me for guidance, strength, and wise insight
Many days you sacrificed
So that others may have and believe in Me
The time has come to release back what you have done daily
Trust
I know your heart
I knew the glory that I would receive from you from the start
Smile

And watch your obedience pay
Receive what is written and the words that I say

The World Shall Know You as My Chosen One!
So let it be written
So let it be done!

THE TURN OF YOUR CENTURY HAS COME!

Just
Because!

Just because people said I couldn't
I did!
No longer keeping my talents hid
Just because they didn't believe
I now achieve!
Just because they thought I wasn't a positive
role model for people to follow
I now lead!
Where they doubted
I now succeed!
And
Just because of you the best has yet
To begin!
JUST
BECAUSE!

No One Is Perfect!

We all make mistakes
But everyone is given an opportunity to redirect their fate
This is what it takes to win
Now let's begin

I can remember that day so vividly
I was standing by the water on a cold winter day
I prayed to the Lord that He take this habit away
I made a promise to my family, my loved ones, and to myself
That I was giving it up to be a better self
And I did for five days
You see, that craving wanted to have its own ways in my life
Then on came the shame
For choosing wrong instead of doing what I knew to be right
Then I found myself questioning my confidence and my might

The Lord Speaks,
I've been waiting for you for so long
To release My Word against your storm
Why do you continue to doubt?
That every trial and tribulation that you embrace
That I, the Lord, can't bring you out!
I know what it feels like to be tempted
I understand that your flesh is weak
But don't you recognize that I gave you the
power to climb into your peak?
Don't you dare claim defeat!
Get up and shake off the dirt

But Lord my Savior it hurts!
Why can't I overcome?
Yet ye of little faith I told you before
that you are My Chosen One!
I The Great I Am
Have written your life plans
I know where and when you are to stand
And take your righteous place on this land

So, God what am I to do?
Hold on, be patient, I will direct you to what is true
All you must do is believe
Believe that I Am able to birth all your dreams
All you must do is be a vessel where My Holy Spirit may dwell
Stop giving glory to hell!

How can You be so forgiving?
How can You love that which forsakes You?
How can You remain so loving and true?

My Child,
How can you forget that I died for you so that
you may have life more abundantly?
How can you forget that I that dwell is also dwelling in you!
You must stop doubting yourself when
you fall short from the mark
You must remember that you moved
further away from your first start
You must remember that this is a process;
nothing will just happen over night

My Child,

It takes time to heal your wounds right!

Walk out on faith

Fall down on your face and continue to give Me

Jesus Christ your highest thanks

For, the battle is already defeated

Victory is yours, now wait and heed it

Get ready

For I, the Lord, shall keep you steady

You have already changed your fate

Just don't get down for I know that all

will continue to make mistakes

You

Listening and Reading

Yes you,

Now

You're living in your breakthrough

As with I, too

You too must be patient with you

NO ONE IS PERFECT

You Are The Chosen One!

Do you want more?
Are you content with your life?
Are you tired of trying when enough never seems right?
Well,
This Is For You And Yes It's True!

I grew up fast
The best of everything I wanted to have
I was beautiful topped with a sexy shape
It was the norm for many to hate
Properly educated, unique, good sense
of humor, and a model look
Made it easy to hook the men
Needless to say, my life was filled with sin
No joke
I loved to get high off that brown sugar smoke
Corona with lemon chasing my Hennessey and coke
Hit the dance floor was all she wrote
I wanted more out of life, seeking my Mr. Right
To capture me from this hell of darkness
and lead me into the light
Yet I felt stuck
Like I had fallen down and was unable to get up
Every day was like the same routine
Trying to wash the dirt away, yet I could never get clean
One thing for sure, I needed and wanted more
Yet my baggage, my demons, were too deep
I knew that a higher power I would have to seek

No less

It was definitely a process, but I finally found a church home
It was in the preacher's words that I started not to feel alone
There were many seeking the same as I
I could hear it in their sorrowful cries
Now don't get me wrong, I was raised up in church
Yet as a child it was fun, now as an adult
the preacher's words started to hurt
I mean I felt the pain
I was tired of living in shame and being satisfied with less
It was time that I was baptized again to achieve my best
Someone told me that before I get baptized, repent
So that all your sins and demons would be brought
back to the owner in which they were sent
So, I kneeled down and asked the Lord for
forgiveness and the strength to live right
Then came my turn to be brought up into the spotlight
Tears fell down my face
As I walked to where the preacher stood for
the water I was about to embrace
I knew that I was about to get washed in the blood of Christ
For He was the offeror and the offering for
His life He did sacrifice for man
So that we may be granted rebirth on this land
I heard the preacher's final words, as I
was pushed into the water of life
I knew that I would never be the same that night
I surrendered myself and my sins were washed away
A brand new me was here to stay
My body felt like I was about to suffocate under
water, for it was hard to get back up

I felt like all my wrong doings and demons were sucked up
And sent to the deepest water, never to return
I swear from that day forward I yearned for God
I yearned to learn the new me
In Christ is where I dwell to be
Yet, I've got to stay true
It wasn't all peaches and cream; I'm
going to keep it real with you
I had to stay in the word
Reading my bible, listening to TD Jakes, and
accepting the knowledge that I heard
I had to cut off a lot of friends
For they were still motivated by sin
I felt lonely sometimes
Going through withdrawal made me
feel like committing a crime
I practice abstinence "Touch Me Not!"
All the negative energy and people I had to drop
Yet, my soul is stronger, my mind is no longer confused
I now recognize my worth and will no
longer allow myself to be used
I make wise choices
I no longer base my self-worth on others' negative voices
I'm free!
I'm finally focusing on me!
I'm still!
I'm allowing my wounds to heal!
I'm working towards my growth goals
The truth, God's grace, I now behold
I no longer need the comfort of a man
I now know who I am and whose I am; on
a firm rock I succeed, I stand!

Now it's my duty to bring God's words and
teachings throughout this land
To you who listens and reads
I plead, if you wish to succeed
You must give God all of you
You must be obedient and follow the truth
For sure,
You said you wanted more
You tried it your way, living day by day
It's time for your rebirth
Before you take your last breath on this Earth
Life!
This is just your test
To determine where your Soul shall forever rest
Heaven or Hell
Triumph or Fail
The choice is yours to make
My Child, you are not a mistake!
Just take one step and God shall take two
It's Time To Walk Into The New You
Amen
So, Let It Be Done
Come to Christ
For
You Are The Chosen One!
It's Time
To Shine
It's Time
The Truth You Shall Find
IT'S TIME!

Dear Man
Dear Brother

There's more to loving than what lies beneath the cover
I need you to hear what I have to say
God said,
"I made you in My own image that first day
Of life
It was I that gave you your greatest gift, your Eve, your wife
Later, I told you to love her as I have loved
My Church which I gave My life for."
My Dearest Man
Tell me,
With your Eve with you, do you help her to become more?
Now dear man,
You're supposed to be the rock in which she stands!
You are her provider here on this land!
Do you treat her as a queen?
Do you spoil her without her having to ask for anything?
Do you pray every day for the blessing that I sent your way?
Do you adore, do you open her door?
Did you provide the home?
Do you make her feel comfortable in those moments
When she feels sad, unattractive, and alone?
Do you greet her with a passionate hug and kiss?
Do you miss her every time that you're apart?
Did you give her all your heart?
Did you tell her that she completes you?
Were you faithful to her and always true?
Did you call? Did you tell all that I found my soul mate?

Did you notice that with her, she helps uplift your fate?

Yes, it takes more to love

As I so did for you!

Did you pray that all her dreams may come true through you?

Notice that your wife becomes your life

She becomes your ministry to cherish and to treasure

One soul, one mind, one body joined together

I hear many of you saying no

Then this is your answer to why your

union didn't grow to maturity

I hope and pray that you hear me

Your soul mate comes but so few

And all along you lose from doing you

It's sad because what she had to offer to you

My Son,

Was Your Break-Through

A virtuous woman is rare to find

To lose her is to lose Me, for we are one of a kind

Don't you see?

She surrendered herself to me

Jesus Christ

I told you that I am your mother, your father,

your sister, your brother, your wife

How I wish you would have done right

Now you must live your lonely life

Now don't get me wrong

There are always women, but she exceeds them all!

Remember one thing before I leave

When you pray for something, and you believe

And I grant it to you

You'd better live for it or else I will take it away from you
Never let a virtuous woman get away
You'd better heed what I say
Today
Dear Man

Dear Brother

I told you before that there's more to loving
then what lies beneath the cover!

Do Right By Our Men!

I HAVE TO SPEAK TO MY SISTERS
AND AS I SPEAK, PLEASE HAVE AN OPEN MIND
FOR, NOW IS THE TIME TO DO RIGHT BY OUR MEN!
NOW LET'S BEGIN

Too often we hear brothers ain't worth it!
Well, today I'm going to contradict this stereotype
You See,
There are many of our brothers living and doing right
You know, I'm going to solve this crime
Like you, I didn't come here to waste any of your time!
SISTERS!
STOP COMPLAINING!
Your man spends more energy on you
Instead of motivating his own dreams to come true!
Stop! Expecting a man to take care of you
To bring happiness into your life
Girl, you'd better get it right!
You will not be happy until you're happy with yourself!
Stop placing your insecurities on someone else!
I know sometimes your neck he wants to grab
Because all you do is nag, nag, nag!
Nagging about what you don't have,
What you need, what you want, what you don't get enough of,
Or too much of, or what you did!
While underneath the truth is hid!
Come on, your mouth is a weapon like a loaded gun
Shot to kill
While every day your man is striving to be someone!

MY SISTERS! We must learn to speak less
To trust that our man's decision is in the best
Of judgment
And if not, don't torment his wrong
My Sisters learn to keep your man strong!
For, the devil attacks the head!
With the burdens of this world attached to the burdens of you
His reasoning becomes confused, then your man is Misled!
Finding peace in another woman's bed!
THE TIME IS NOW. MY SISTERS, USE YOUR HEAD!
Be honest with yourself
For, if you choose to stay the
Complaining Must Stop!
If not,
Drop that brother before you're loving in sin!
Meditate On This Message My Sisters
For, The Time Is Now To Do

RIGHT BY OUR MEN!
Here's A Clue:

IT WILL ONLY BEGIN WHEN
YOU DO RIGHT BY YOU!

My Daughter

This may not come the way you expected, but it's true
Stop settling for less and do right by you
You can work, but what are you working for?
Will this job bridge you to more?
Then why waste time?
Pay close attention for the truth you shall find
It's more than men
It's more than laying down in sin
When will you learn?
That love is earned, not freely given!
Stop living for materialistic things
Stop feigning for a wedding ring
To rescue you
It is you that must break your breakthrough
It is you that must make your dreams come true
So, why wait?
It's been years and you haven't found your soulmate
So let the truth be found
What goes around, comes around
Watch your friends
Watch how you make your ends
Meet
Watch how you present yourself in the streets
And destiny you shall meet
Well, it's close to an end
So, how long will you live in those sins?
Come wholeheartedly to Me
Jesus your Christ, your Almighty

And I will wash you clean
I will give you a new tune to sing
I will be the man of your dreams
As the lady at the well
Can I have a drink? *(John 4:7-42)*
For what I come to give is living water!
God chose you and claimed you as His own

MY DAUGHTER

Chapter 7

WE ARE AT WAR!

"Be transformed by the renewing of your mind." (Romans 12:2)

"Finally, brothers and sisters, whatever is true, whatever is noble, whatever is right, whatever is pure, whatever is lovely, whatever is admirable - if anything is excellent or praiseworthy – think about such things" (Philippians 4:8)

"The weapons we fight with are not the weapons of the world. On the contrary, they have divine power to demolish strongholds. We demolish arguments and every pretension that sets itself up against the knowledge of God, and we take captive every thought to make it obedient to Christ." (2 Corinthians 10:4 NIV)

"Thus, saith the Lord unto you, be not afraid nor dismayed by reason of this great multitude; for the battle is not yours, but God's." (2 Chronicles 20:15 NIV)

You Can't Serve Two Masters

A Doubleminded Man Is Unstable in All His Ways

This is your warning. You'd better heed what the Word says

To You

We're going to sweep through

The talk and get straight to the facts

How you speak and the way you act

You say you love Me, but as soon as I turn my back

You fall once again off track

What do you want from Me?

I placed in you everything that is needed

to make your dreams a reality

But you expect Me to also do all the work

Then what were you needed for when I created man out of dirt

I did, but what have you done?

I spent more time cleaning up your wild nights of fun

I comfort you when love left; it was I that held your hand

It was My Self-Sacrifice that gave you life on this land

Yet, you deny Me!

Many times, I told you to drop that deadly habit

To labor for My Will

Many days I healed

I covered you in My Blood

Yet, you too have a love for sin

You too love the fast life which leads to a dead end

My strength is made perfect in your weakness

Therefore, death can never win

It has to loose you!

This here is your breakthrough!
Instill what has been written on this page!

A DOUBLEMINDED MAN IS
UNSTABLE IN ALL HIS WAYS!

You know I often hear many of the lame
Complain
About their trials and tribulations
But I'll tell you the truth
If only you knew
What awaits you
At the end of the test
I too confess

I Had To Go Through

In order to learn what JESUS already knew
About my personal relationship with Him and how He sees me
What I speak is destiny
I Tell You Love Thy Enemies
I had to go through a severe bodily injury
to know JESUS as my Healer
I had to lose everything I had to understand Him as my Builder
I had to be baptized in His Blood to know that He is my Savior
I had to lose all my old friends to comprehend
that He too is a Good Neighbor
I had to go without money for many days
to be able to call Him my Provider
I had to hear my Word to know that Satan is a liar!
This is for you
I need you to receive what is true
In order to have your breakthrough
You have to kill the old you and let JESUS through
The time is now
Child, let the truth be found!
I had to be without men

To receive JESUS as my Husband
I had to be fatherless to be known as my Daughter
I had to drop my water pots to know Christ as my Living Water
I had to surrender to know Him as my
Master, my Good Shepherd
To call Him My Father, My Brother
I had to be without love to know that He too is my Lover!
Hold tight
It's going to be all right
I declare in the Name of Jesus balance over your life
Do Right
Turn it over to Christ!
I had to go through a nervous breakdown to
know Him as my Good Counselor
To be able to call Him my Friend
I had to accept the Word to know JESUS
as my Beginning and my End
I had to sin
To be able to call Him my Redeemer, my
Deliverer, my King of kings
I had to go through in order for my praise to have a tune to sing
Unto my Lord
You see, the more You go through
The more you discover just how much Christ is in love with you!
I tell you, in order to find what is true
I had to
And so do you
We all have to go through!
Yet, I promise you at the end of the test
CHRIST is waiting for YOU!

I Had To Go Through
In order to learn what JESUS already knew
About my personal relationship with Him and how He sees me
What I speak is destiny
I Tell You Love Thy Enemies
But, on the real, stop letting people get to you
Control your emotions
What you don't kill, will kill you
Stop denying what you already know as true
Stop dreaming of the break, but breakthrough
Only God can help you off the ground
You down
Give it to CHRIST. Let Him direct your life
This is your night
COME!
ALL ARE WELCOME!

To Be A Leader For Christ!

KEEP YOUR HEAD UP HIGH!
Don't you dare cry!
Who told you that the road was easy?
Who told you that you wouldn't have
to pay a cost to free the lost?
That you wouldn't have to pay a price
TO BE A LEADER FOR CHRIST!

HEAR WHAT IS SAID
Pick up your Head!
Stand tall!
You learn
You grow stronger with each fall!

MANY
Many fought the battle before you
Died for justice
Tortured for speaking what was true

HERE YOU SIT!
Not appreciating it!
Head down
Depressed, weak-minded, dreaming of a better day
Yet, not willing to fight for your crown!
For Sure!
THIS IS WAR!

THE STORM
THE BATTLE
Has reached its peak
The secret to victory is to improve the
areas in you that are weak!
THE SECRET TO VICTORY IS TO IMPROVE
THE AREAS IN YOU THAT ARE WEAK!

WHILE YOU STRIVE
Don't you dare quit or cry!
Finish the race!
In which so many before you had to embrace!

YOU'RE NOT
LIVING FOR YOU
You're just a piece of the puzzle brought forth to birth
GOD'S WILL
Heaven on Earth!

STOP!
LIVING FOR THINGS!
Cars, clothes, jewelry, and diamond rings
Stand and claim!
RIGHTEOUS IN JESUS' NAME!

LIKE THE STORM
MY TIME HERE IS NOT LONG

Dry your tears
Stop living in fear
Victory is near!

WALK PROUD AMONGST ANY CROWD
Forgive and love your enemies
Yet, beware of the enemy in me

KEEP YOUR HEAD UP HIGH!
It's time to move until you die!
Recognize your strength!
Bow down and give thanks!

CLAIM!
WALK EVER FORWARD IN JESUS' NAME!

KEEP YOUR HEAD UP HIGH!
Don't you dare quit or cry!
Who told you that the road was easy?
Who told you that you wouldn't have
to pay a cost to free the lost?
That you wouldn't have to pay a price

TO BE A LEADER FOR CHRIST!

MESSIAH
YOUR FAITHFUL LOVE ENDURES FOREVER

From The Depths Of Despair,

O Lord, I call for your help
Hear my cry, O Lord pay attention to my prayer
This year I will live in my true worth
For, *my help comes from the Lord who made Heaven and Earth*
Savior, I now cast away all my worries and all my cares
For scripture says,
The Lord is for me, so I will have no fear
What can mere people do to me?
I will look in triumph at those who hate me
My destiny is now made into my daily reality!
I will labor to be all that I was called to be
For, *in my distress I prayed to the Lord and*
the Lord answered and set me free
I tell you, all day He watches over me
In His army I received my number
He will not let me stumble, the one who
watches over me will not slumber
His unfailing mercy towards me will not fade
For, *the Lord himself watches over me*
The Lord stands beside me as my protective shade
His Holy Spirit leads me to right
For, *the Lord keeps me from all harm and watches over my life*
Our souls are immersed together
For, *the Lord keeps watch over me as I*
come and go, both now and forever

I tell you no lie

Lord, if you kept a record of our sins who,

O Lord, could ever survive?

But you offer forgiveness that we might learn to fear you

Yet, this is true

Lord it's through Your Blood that we were

able to receive our breakthrough

To the world, it's time to use our common sense

For, *it is better to take refuge in the Lord*

than to trust in people and in prince

O World, hope in the Lord for with the Lord there

is unfailing love, his redemption overflows

He himself will redeem us from every kind of sin

Yet, you must first welcome Jesus in!

This is our year of more!

For, as the waters fill the sea, so the Earth will

be filled with people who know the Lord

I was sent here to share!

That the Lord heard you

FROM THE DEPTHS OF YOUR DESPAIR!

I'm Going To Praise You!

In Spite of

The GREAT I AM THAT I AM I'm going to give you love

In spite of no money to pay the bills

In spite of responsibilities stacked like hills

In spite of dead-end relationships and friends

In spite of struggling to meet my ends

In spite of the shame and guilt

In spite of being surrounded by filth

I'm going to say Hallelujah my Lord and Savior

Hallelujah for being such a Good Neighbor

Hallelujah, Jesus Christ

Hallelujah for Your Blood that saved my soul's life

You see,

I fear not, for my Father holds my destiny

I walk by faith, not by sight

In spite of the smoke screen, I still see the light

I know for sure that this is real

God is returning back double fold what the devil tried to steal

What he tried to kill

FatherGodSpirit make me now whole and healed!

It's a new day

I may

Be without

But, in spite of everything I'm still going to shout

Hallelujah even before I make my way out!

For, what I feel is an everlasting true!

Lord, in spite of, even after, death

I'M GOING TO PRAISE YOU!

I Speak

That I am strengthened in those areas that are weak
I speak victory!
I speak that the Power of God flows through me
I have reached beyond the stars
To tell you that the Glory of the Lord is ours
By faith
By Jesus, Son of God's Name
All that is purposed for me, I claim!
I do
What I was called to
I know unconditional love
I know about the mercy and grace sent from above
I work life
I live
I am empowered to unfailingly give
My seeds are like the fertilizer of this Earth
God has revealed my true worth
I smile
For this one life I take not for granted
I sow what the Lord has planted
And do know
That after this life, my soul to Heaven will go
Greeted with the highest honor of them all
The wife of the reason that healed our downfall
Mrs. Christ
I live now to announce that He is the ruler of my Life
It may not be perfect right now
But I tell you that the truth of these words will be found

For I come not to just live

But to leave a mark that no man can cover

I come to the Glory, our Forever Lover

The GREAT I AM

Raise me into Your Spirit

For, I say yes!

I AM a Child of God brought forth to strengthen what is weak!

I AM One with The Lord

I Speak

There is no stopping me!

Jesus Wept

JUST FOR YOU!

Let the words of my mouth and the meditation
of my heart be acceptable in thy sight, O Lord
my Strength, my Redeemer, my Holy True
Excuse me, let me come through
You see, I was sent here to deliver a Word just for you!

It's time to speak the Word over your situation
God is our refuge and strength, a very present help
in trouble. So, ride the waves with patience.
I have been young, and now am old
Yet, I have not seen the righteous forsaken, nor
his seed begging bread. So let it be told:
Get in the groove!
Cast thy burden upon the Lord and He shall sustain thee,
He shall never suffer the righteous to be moved!
And we know that all things work together
for good to them that love God,
To them who are the called according to
his purpose. So, stand in faith!
Through the pain, don't complain, but give God thanks!
I tell you no lie
I waited patiently for the Lord, and he
inclined unto me and heard my cry
He hears you, too
You see, Jesus wept just for you to live again
The Lord is my Shepherd. I shall not
want, for He died for all my sins

It gets so hard sometimes, I too confess
And I said, O that I had wings like a dove for
then I would fly away and be at rest
But, my God said,
Be still and know that I AM GOD; I will be exalted
among the nations. I will be exalted in the Earth!
This is Your Confirmation that You Will Live in Your Worth!
THE STORM NOW IN OUR LORD'S BLOOD IS KEPT
HE HEARD YOUR CRY AND JESUS WEPT

Order My Steps In Your Word!

LORD!

I PRAY THESE WORDS ARE HEARD!

Not a driven

But

A directed life I seek to find

LORD

A line

My steps direct me to what is next to claim

In

JESUS' NAME!

FATHER

I apologize for the amount of time it

took me to realize my worth

Through Rebirth,

The true reason to bring Heaven here on Earth

I WAS LOST

DYING FOR SIN

Soaked in misery, struggling each day to win

Back my peace of mind

My thirst for what life brings

Now, through CHRIST'S Blood

Like my ancestors, the liberty bell rings!

MASTER

MY SOUL

I SOLD TO YOU

For,

It's in Your Word that I uphold to be true!

USE ME LORD!

For,

I'm not afraid of the process!

USE ME LORD!

For,

At the end of the storm, I shall be blessed!

USE ME LORD!

Order My Steps In Your Word

USE ME LORD!

I Pray These Words Are Heard!

USE ME LORD!

Sight Me On What I See!

I PRAY

DIRECT MY STEPS!

L O R D U S E M E !

I Love The Person That
I Have Become!

I LOVE EVEN MORE WHAT IS TO COME

GOD'S CHOSEN ONE

Self-motivated

Giving continuous glory for, without

God, I wouldn't have made it

In that cocoon

I was being transformed like a baby in its mother's womb

Loneliness and self-doubt

Embracing pain to break out

To break free

And live in what you were meant to be

There's no one quite like me

Through the tears

Push

Through the fears

Push

Push until your birth

Now is, you're living in your true worth!

I apologize

For the amount of time

It took me to get here

But thank God I'm here

Able to share

Another day

It's amazing how we don't appreciate things

Until they're taken away

Heed what I say
On this day
What was of the past
Shall no longer last
What once blocked your way
Became your stepping stone today
It adds to your life story
To your testimony to come!
In the meantime, speak it by faith that
I Love The Person That I Have Become!

I'm All Woman

Still coming
In spite of the pain
Still working hard to claim
My destiny
ALL WOMAN, I hope you hear me

You've been through
But, ALL WOMAN, this was meant for the best of you!
And it's true
This is your season of birth
This is your moment to labor for your true worth
My Vibrant Daughter
Get your priorities in order
It's yours to have
Just grab
Your blessings
Now is, learn from your daily lessons!
ALL WOMAN just be
The best that you can be
See your future, write it plain
Claim it in Jesus' Matchless Name
And watch you grow
I promise you; the old you people won't know
ALL WOMAN, let it go!

Step out on something you never did before
You have to sometimes lose in order to gain more
Time is not to waste

Make wiser your paste
Steer away from this world's rat race
The truth: Your time has come.
So let it be done!
Claim

I'M ALL WOMAN!

THE WORLD IS MINE
THIS IS MY TIME TO SHINE

This Is My Season For Change!

Yes, it may feel strange
For some time
But, with all that I am and will become,
I shall let my light shine
For scripture said,
"That I am not the tail but the head"
That for everything there is a season
A time to be born and a time to die
No longer shall I live a lie
A time to kill and time to heal
I will allow God's Holy Spirit to instill His Will
A time to tear down and a time to build up
And up is my attitude, no longer shall I be stuck
You see, enough is enough!
I have to stretch my arms and allow my soul to be set free
I am now in control of birthing my own destiny
Turning my dreams into my daily reality
And fear and defeat no longer live. I will give
What it takes to succeed
Where others doubted or left
I will pick up the pieces and believe
It's been hard, but this great pain
Will bring forth an abundant gain
In my life
What the devil meant for evil will be made holy and right

I shout, "No more strife!"

I will welcome each brand-new day that I am blessed to see

I will welcome my mind, body, and soul

To fall back in love with me

You see, I am a new creature

I will make a difference on this Earth

From this day forward, I live and flourish in my true worth

You may wonder why I don't cry, but keep a smile on my face

You may wonder how this new joy and laughter I embrace

Well, there is a reason!

I told you before

THIS IS MY SEASON!

I've Got Murder On My Mind!

SPEAK THAT

TO COUNTERACT

THE ENEMY EVERY TIME!

*For we wrestle not against flesh and blood, but
against principalities, against powers, against the
rulers of the darkness of this world, against spiritual
wickedness in high places (Ephesians 6:12)*

But God's Living Word chases

The enemy, freeing all men, women, boys, and girls

For, *You are from God, little children, and have
overcome them; because greater is He who is in
you than he who is in the world (1 John 4:4)*

I'VE GOT MURDER ON MY MIND I CRY

When the enemy arises

Trying to deceive you with lies

Stand on God's Word to Break Through!

*Behold, I have given you authority to tread on serpents
and scorpions; and over all the power of the enemy,
and nothing shall hurt you! (Luke 10:19)*

*Therefore, do not let sin reign in your mortal body, that you
should obey it in its lusts. For sin shall not have dominion over
you, for you are not under law but under grace (Romans 6:12-14)*

This truth I need you to meditate on

and wholeheartedly embrace

*For, we know that our old sinful selves were crucified with Christ
so that sin might lose its power in our lives. We are no longer
slaves to sin. For when we died with Christ, we were set free from
the power of sin. And since we died with Christ, we know we will*

also live with him. We are sure of this because Christ was raised from the dead, and he will never die again. Death no longer has any power over him. When he died, he died once to break the power of sin. But now he lives, he lives for the Glory of God. So, you also should consider yourselves to be dead to the power of sin and alive to God through Christ Jesus (Romans 6: 6-11)

If God be for us who or what can be against us

Only in Christ Jesus do we place our trust

For God *made Him who knew no sin to be sin on our behalf; so that we might become the righteousness of God in Him*

I shout if you want to overcome sin!

Whatsoever things are true, whatsoever things are honest, whatsoever things are just, whatsoever things are pure, whatsoever things are lovely, whatsoever things are of good report; if there be any virtue, and if there be any praise, think on these things (Philippians 4:8)

And God will give you a new song to sing

For Blessed is a man who perseveres under trial; for once he has been approved, he will receive the crown of life which the Lord has promised to those who love Him (James 1:12)

SPEAK I'VE GOT MURDER ON MY MIND TO OVERCOME SIN!

For the thief comes only to steal and kill and destroy. I came that they may have life and have it abundantly (John 10:10)

I hope you hear me!

For though we live in the world, we do not wage war as the world does. The weapons we fight with are not the weapons of the world. On the contrary, they have divine power to demolish strongholds. We demolish arguments and every pretension that

sets itself up against the knowledge of God, and we take captive
every thought to make it obedient to Christ (2 Cor. 10:3-5)

When in a fight!

Put on the full armor of God, so that when the day of evil comes,
you may be able to stand your ground, and after you have done
everything, to stand. Stand firm then, with the belt of truth
buckled around your waist, with the breastplate of righteousness
in place, and with your feet fitted with the readiness that comes
from the gospel of peace. In addition to all this, take up the
shield of faith, with which you can extinguish all the flaming
arrows of the evil one. Take the helmet of salvation and the
sword of the Spirit, which is the word of God (Eph. 6: 11-17)

And watch how God returns abundantly
what the enemy tried to rob

For not by might nor by power, but by My
Spirit says the Lord of hosts

Do we boost

In

I'VE GOT MURDER ON MY MIND AND IT'S KILLING
WHILE I'M WALKING INTO A NEW BEGIN

I want to help you, too!

Submit therefore to God. Resist the devil and he will flee from
you. Draw near to God and He will draw near to you. Cleanse
your hands, you sinners; and purify your hearts, you double-
minded. Be miserable and mourn and weep; let your laughter be
turned into mourning and your joy to gloom. Humble yourselves
in the presence of the Lord, and He will exalt you! (James 4 7:10)

For, if we say that we have fellowship with Him and yet walk
in the darkness; we lie and do not practice the truth; but if
we walk in the Light as He Himself is in the Light, we have

fellowship with one another, and the blood of Jesus His Son
cleanses us from all sin. If we say that we have no sin, we are
deceiving ourselves and the truth is not in us. If we confess
our sins. He is faithful and righteous to forgive us our sins
and to cleanse us from all unrighteousness (1 John 1: 6-9)

FatherGodSpirit I need you to hear this!

Create in me a clean heart, O God and renew a
steadfast spirit within me (Psalm 51:10)

You see,

We all stumble in many ways (James 3:2)
I want to do what is good, but I don't. I don't want to do
what is wrong, but I do it anyway (Romans 7 19-20)
Bend down, O Lord, and hear my prayer; answer me, for I need
your help (Psalm 86:1) Restore to me the joy of your salvation
and grant me a willing spirit, to sustain me (Psalm 51:12)

My Brothers and Sisters here's the key!

Pray without ceasing. In everything give thanks for this is the will
of God in Christ Jesus concerning you (1 Thessalonians 4: 17-18)

Here's another Word that I want you to hold on to

For, no temptation has overtaken you except what is
common to humanity. God is faithful, and He will not
allow you to be tempted beyond what you are able, but
with the temptation He will also provide a way of escape
so that you are able to bear it (1 Corinthians 10:13)
Therefore, put to death your members which are on the
Earth: fornication, uncleanness, passion, evil desire,
and covetousness, which is idolatry (Colossians 3:5)

I'm telling you that the Word of God is Your Victory!

Since Christ suffered for us in the flesh, arm yourselves also with
the same mind, for he who has suffered in the flesh has ceased

from sin, that he no longer should live the rest of his time in the
flesh for the lusts of men, but for the Will of God (1 Peter 4: 1-2)

I want reading the Bible, feeding on the
Word's feast, to be your daily job

For him who overcomes Jesus said I will grant to sit
with Me on My throne, as I also overcame and sat down
with My Father on His throne (Revelation 3:21)

Walk by the Spirit, and you will not carry out the
desire of the flesh for God alone (Gal. 5:16)

Is your rock and fortress that will never be shaken
Lord Your Word I have treasured in my heart that
I may not sin against You (Psalm 119:11)

I'VE GOT MURDER ON MY MIND AND
THE ENEMY CAN'T GET THROUGH

For if anyone is in Christ, he is a new creature; the old things
passed away; behold, new things have come (2 Corinthians 5:17)

Hear me, My Chosen One

For we do not have a High Priest who cannot sympathize
with our weaknesses, but was in all points tempted as
we are, yet without sin. Let us therefore come boldly to
the throne of grace, that we may obtain mercy and find
grace to help in time of need (Hebrews 4: 15-16)

My Child of God, in this do believe

That he who dwells in the shelter of the Most High will rest in
the shadow of the Almighty. I will say of the Lord, He is my
refuge and my fortress, my God, in whom I trust. Surely, he will
save you from the fowler's snare and from the deadly pestilence.
He will cover you with his feathers, and under his wings you will
find refuge; his faithfulness will be your shield (Ps. 91: 1-4)

I'VE GOT MURDER ON MY MIND FOR GOD'S WORD DOES HEAL

For you have girded me with strength for battle; You have
subdued under me those who rose up against me (Ps 18:39)
I Just Used the Word of God to Conquer All My Enemies
I overcame my threats
For, I have conquered him by the blood of the
Lamb and by the Word of my testimony, for I loved
not my life even unto death (Rev. 12:11)
I decree and declare this word over our neighborhoods
Do not be overcome with evil but overcome
evil with good! (Rom 12:21)
Pass God's Word to every man, woman, boy, and girl
For I have told you these things, so that in me you may
have peace. In this world you will have trouble. But
take heart! I have overcome the world (John 16:33)
And you will know the truth, and the truth will set you free
"I'VE GOT MURDER ON MY MIND," I SHOUT.
"SPEAK THE WORD OF GOD CONTINUOUSLY!"
Do not fear them, for the Lord your God is the one fighting
for you. Have I not commanded you? Be strong and
courageous! Do not tremble or be dismayed, for the Lord
your God is with you wherever you go (Josh 1:9) So, do
not be afraid or discouraged because of this vast army.
For the battle is not yours, but God's (Chron. 20:15)
So, when the enemy, even the enemy that lives
in me, standS up to steal, kill, or rob
The Word of God I Will Make My Stand
Why? When we belong to Christ, the enemy never has the
final word over our lives. We are secure in God's hands

Therefore, when temptation ariseS
To entice you through your flesh, pride, and eyes
I need you to repeat these words every time!
Devil, you are already defeated because

I'VE GOT MURDER ON MY MIND!

The Word of GOD Wins Every time!
Murder On My Mind!
Katrina T. Smith

Do You Want to Be Healed?

I gave you the answer, I pulled you out of the pit, I drew
you out of deep waters yet like a dog returning to his vomit
to eat it again, you return right back to that which kills!
DO YOU WANT TO BE HEALED?

Then *My Child, be attentive to my words; incline your ear
to my sayings. Do not let them escape from your sight; keep
them within your heart. For they are life to those who find
them, and healing to all their flesh (Proverbs 4:20-22)*

I confess

Get up! Pick up your mat and walk (John 5:8)

For your actions speaks louder than your talk

It's been years

And you're still struggling with the same

doubts, strongholds, lack, and fears

DO YOU WANT TO BE HEALED!

Then the Word of God must be instilled

Within You!

For only through Christ Jesus do you make it through

For, *surely he has borne our infirmities and carried our
diseases; yet we accounted him stricken, struck down by God,
and afflicted. But he was wounded for our transgressions,
crushed for our iniquities; upon him was the punishment
that made us whole, and by his bruises we are whole*

So, let it be told

*"Bless the Lord, O my soul, and do not forget all his benefits-
who forgives all your iniquity, who heals all your diseases, who*

redeems your life from the Pit, who crowns you with steadfast love and mercy, who satisfies you with good as long as you live so that your youth is renewed like the eagle's," I shout!
The Word of GOD is your way out!

Can These Dead Bones Live Again?

LISTEN!
The Hand of the Lord is on me and by
His Spirit **I come to give more!**
Dry bones, hear the Word of the Lord!
I will make breath enter you, and you will come to life!
Come, breath, from the four winds and breathe
into these dead bones that they may live **for Our**
Sovereign Lord JESUS our CHRIST!

I speak to your Soul
For now is your time to be whole
I command in the Name of JESUS all
unclean spirits to come out of you!
That strongholds, generational curses, diseases,
suicidal thoughts, and lack has to loose you too!
For God has given me authority to tread on serpents
and scorpions, and over all the power of the enemy
And nothing shall hurt me!
For those that believe!
JESUS said in *My Name they will cast out demons and speak*
in new tongues. **Only by their faith in Me shall they succeed!**
In the Sovereign Name of *JESUS, I call out all these evils*
which defile a person for it is from within, out of a person's
heart, that evil thoughts come – sexual immorality, theft,
murder, adultery, greed, malice, deceit, lewdness, envy,
slander, arrogance, and folly, I shout! (Mark 7: 20)
Today is YOUR cleanse; no longer shall you live in fear,
guilt, shame, worry, sorrow, hatred, and self-doubt!

Have mercy on me, O God, according to your
unfailing love; according to your great compassion,
blot out my transgressions. Wash away all my iniquity
and cleanse me from my sin (Psalm 51:1-2)

All Power Rests in Our Beginning and Our End!

Jesus said, "I am the way, and the truth, and the life. No
one comes to the Father except through me." (John 14:6)

Lord of Heaven's Armies!

Your God, Your Almighty!

Therefore, if anyone is in Christ, he or she is a new creation.
The old has passed away; behold the new has come

From this Day Forward the World Shall
Know You As God's Chosen One!

For scripture says, "But you are a chosen race, a royal
priesthood, a holy nation, a people for His own possession,
that you may proclaim the excellences of Him who called
you out of darkness into His marvelous light (1 Peter 2:9)

From this day forward I will live Christ-like!

Follow the pattern of the sound Words that you have heard
from me, in the faith and love that are in Christ Jesus
For, if God is for us who or what can be against us!

Speak and believe this daily!

That I have been crucified with Christ and I no longer
live, but Christ lives in me. The life I now live in the
body, I live by faith in the Son of God, who loved
me and gave Himself for me (Galatians 2:20)

You see, through the Blood of Jesus I now live in victory!
CAN THESE DEAD BONES LIVE AGAIN?
YES! BY YOUR FAITH! PLEASE HEAR
ME! LET THESE WORDS IN!

The Hand of the Lord is on me and by
His Spirit I come to give more!
Repent then turn to God, so that your sins may be wiped out,
that times of refreshing may come from the Lord (Acts 3:19)
Let the redeemed of the LORD tell their story (Psalm 107:2)
May you live each day and hereafter to give God glory
For today, you have been raised from the dead
Now, Led
By the Holy Spirit you are reborn to win!
DEAR CHILDREN OF GOD, NO MORE CAN
THESE DEAD BONES LIVE AGAIN!

Daddy's Home

I decree and declare that God alone

Is my rock and my salvation my fortress where

I will never be shaken! (Psalm 62:2)

It has taken

Some time

For the TRUTH to find

Yet, PRAISE GOD that you are here!

Now able to share

In the Fruits of the Spirit

I tell you only through reading the Bible, meditating on

the Word, and living out what is heard do you receive it!

Today, you made a choice to live a new way

You surrendered your own wants, needs,

and desires to God's Will

By reading, by eating, and by seeking after

the Word, God's Power was instilled

It cut through

And made a new you!

God's voice, you can hear it

You are now led by the Holy Spirit

There is no more feeling empty, lost, and alone!

God heard your loud tone and told me to

tell you that **DADDY'S HOME!**

Amen! Holy Spirit I Welcome You in! Amen!

I GOT THIS!

GOD said, just sit back for this you don't want to miss

Turning water into wine

Saving souls one day at a time

Raising the dead

Helping others choose Jesus Christ instead

Prosperity

Beyond your daily need

My Child of GOD you were created to succeed!

In all things know deep within

Yes, even over all your sins

That you are destined to win!

Fear not, bad habits drop

For the time has come, GOD has risen from HIS seat

To conquer all that which keeps you in defeat

According to HIS WILL

In Jesus Christ's Matchless Name all things are healed

You are made whole for this victory, only

GOD could use HIS MIGHTY FIST!

So, rest assured that GOD said, I GOT THIS!

God has now revealed to us his mysterious plan regarding Christ, a plan to fulfill His own good pleasure. And this is the plan. At the right time He will bring everything together under the authority of Christ – everything in Heaven and on Earth. Furthermore, because we are united with Christ, we have received an inheritance from God, for He chose us in advance, and he makes everything work out according to his plan. (Ephesians 1:9-11)

This Message Is Meant for Every Man!

L i s t e n !

I Need You to Slow Down "Peace Be
Still!" and pay close attention!
For What I Speak Is an Everlasting Truth
GOD HIMSELF HAS HIS HAND ON YOU!
You were born for a reason
If I can say just for this season
To STAND
To make your positive difference on this land
We are all stronger together
GOD'S GREATEST CREATION, MAN, standing
side by side through all kinds of weather
We must LOVE MORE, LOVE UNFAILINGLY
To defeat the enemy, even the enemy in me
It's time to live out your true destiny
On this Earth
Before your body returns to dirt
Stay Alert!
For the enemy only comes but to steal, kill, and rob
But God!
Is Greater!

In this season I decree and declare that we will show more understanding, compassion, and love to all our neighbors!
All Your Sisters and Brothers!
We were created to love one another!
So, here's our stand!
God has givEN you unlimited power according to your ability, capacity, will, sacrifice, faith, and works, all which are needed to succumb and overtake this land!
Believe not what you daily see
In spite of the negativity
Still believe more in God's unfailing favor and power
For, this is your hour!
Dry your tears
Stop being motivated by other people and
your own thoughts and fears
Speak, "I Don't Care About Your
Negative Actions and Words."
LISTEN!
FOR, THIS JUST HAD TO BE HEARD!
YOU ARE THE CHOSEN ONE
YES, YOU, MY DEAR DAUGHTER AND DEAR SON
IT'S TIME!
FROM THIS DAY FORWARD "THE
TRUTH" YOU SHALL FIND!

L I S T E N!

I Need You to Slow Down "Peace Be
Still!" and pay close attention!

God has now revealed to us his mysterious plan regarding Christ, a plan to fulfill His own good pleasure. And this is the plan. At the right time He will bring everything together under the authority of Christ – everything in Heaven and on Earth. Furthermore, because we are united with Christ, we have received an inheritance from God, for He chose us in advance, and he makes everything work out according to his plan. (Ephesians 1:9-11)
This Message Is Meant for Every Man!

L I S T E N!

AND GO WORK GOD'S PLAN!

FOR SURE!

WE ARE AT WAR!

We Are at War!

When going to war with temptation
I want you to observe how JESUS brought
forth Satan's damnation
You've got to speak the Word on it!
For we are not fighting against people made of flesh and blood
We are at War for the GOD that dwells above
Step in the Name of Love!

It's time to reclaim
What the Devil stole in Jesus' Name
It's time to fight
For our birthright
Zion break through tonight
Put your hands up
Shout enough is enough!
Don't let anything hold you back, for sure
Lift your head up high, get ready to fight
We Are at War!!

I know what others have to say about me
Yet, I AM a CHILD OF GOD, so the
scripture is my only true reality
To my so-called enemies!
Scripture says, no weapon formed against me shall
prosper. Look God has given me authority over all the
power of the enemy. I can walk amongst snakes and
scorpions and crush them; nothing will injure me!

Why, because the Word stays on my mind
and in my soul constantly!

And to my trials and tribulations
To my storms and this hateful nation!
Scripture says, what is impossible for me, is possible with God
So, my finances shall flourish where others tried to rob
My dreams shall come true
For, scripture says, that your faith has healed you!

It's time to reclaim
What the Devil stole in Jesus' Name
It's time to fight
For our birthright
Zion's breakthrough is tonight
Put your hands up
Shout enough is enough!
Don't let anything hold you back, for sure
Lift your head up high, get ready to fight
We Are at War!

And to those who laugh, talk trash, and stab in order to win!
Scripture says that I will take my place in the Kingdom of God
Where some who seem least important
now will be the greatest then!
You see,
I was reborn to win!
And to those speaking on my sins!
Yes, you who have so much to say!

Scripture says that there is more joy in Heaven over one lost
sinner who repents and returns to God than over ninety-
nine who are righteous and haven't strayed away!
So, you'd better watch what you say!
Before the wrath of God comes your way!
Go ahead and throw dirt
Hit me where it hurts
Turn your backs
Push me off track
I'm loved all by my own!
Yet, remember that the stone that the builders have
rejected has now become the cornerstone!

It's time to reclaim
What the Devil stole in Jesus' Name
It's time to fight
For our birthright
Zion break through tonight
Put your hands up
Shout enough is enough!
Don't let anything hold you back, for sure
Lift your head up high, get ready to fight
We Are at War!!

I know who I AM and whose I AM and
what others have to say about me!
But I told you before that I AM a Child of GOD
so the scripture is my only true reality!
Who cares what you have to say about ME!

It's time to reclaim
What the Devil stole in Jesus Name
It's time to fight
For our birthright
Zion break through tonight
Put your hands up
Shout enough is enough!
Don't let nothing hold you back, for sure
Lift your head up high, get ready to fight
We Are at War!

I'm Willing to Pay the Price!

I want to lay myself on the altar as a living sacrifice
I want the congregation to speak good fortune,
long-suffering, and strength over my life
I want my family to attend my funeral, for the old me has died
Died in order for Christ to arrive
For Christ to revive
My dry bones
This is my life I give to Christ alone
I welcome the change
I welcome the moments when everything around
me seems out of order and strange
I welcome the peace in the midst of the storm
I welcome the test, for this mess, too, won't last long!
I WELCOME YOU
CHILDREN OF GOD TO THE ONE WHO
IS CALLED SO HOLY SO TRUE
I welcome you, too
To experience your breakthrough
All you have to say
"Is give it to me Lord now
Let your truth be found whole in my soul
For I believe

That because of Your Blood I will succeed
I am free
Thank you, Savior, for welcoming me
Into Eternal Life
I confess JESUS as my CHRIST

I too want to lay myself on the altar as a living sacrifice
I too am willing to pay the price
Call Me a Follower of CHRIST!

Something is going to happen to "YOU" tonight
This I speak into your life
Amen
Let the Victory Begin
Deny Sin to Win
Pay the Price!
SURRENDER TO JESUS CHRIST!

My Life, My Life Has Been Changed
My life, my life, my life, my life has been changed!
All around me is rearranged
Since I Met the Lord I Will Never Be the Same
A new, I'm a new creature is Christ Jesus
AMEN! LET THE VICTORY BEGIN!

BISHOP KATRINA T. SMITH

"YOUR QUEEN"

(BEST KEPT SECRET REVEALED)

Bishop Katrina T. Smith aka K.T.S "The Truth" is our 21st century poetry in motion. Her authentic, powerful, and creative use of words inspire while challenging action from the reader. Katrina is the next Langston Hughes and Maya Angelou rebirthed in our generation. Her live performances bring to life each word spoken through a teachable approach. You can read, listen, and purchase more of this dynamic poet's works at <u>itjusthadtobeheard.com</u>.

So, Who is the Lady Behind the Word?

Bishop Katrina T. Smith is a native from Trenton and Hamilton, New Jersey. She holds double degrees in Education and Psychology from Rider University in Lawrenceville, New Jersey. In 2010, she graduated with high honors from Jones International University receiving her master's degree in Education Administration. She is currently in the final process of obtaining her Doctor of Education in Organizational Leadership with an Emphasis in K-12 Leadership. Katrina was recently consecrated as a Bishop.

This unique business professional founded Raising Young Ladies and Men, a program that challenges the youth to pursue excellence in all areas of their lives. Katrina also founded It Just Had To Be Heard, a ministry dedicated to pushing out the Word of God, unifying all races, and calling all individuals to grow into what they were created to do! This long-awaited ministry uses the healing power of poetry combined with music, books, clothing, and art to inspire and motivate all! You can listen and purchase Katrina's flip on poetry CD titled "We Are At War" at itjusthadtobeheard.com gift section.

Katrina quotes, "Life is filled with trials and tribulations, loss and gain, joy, and pain. Yet, one thing remains true. Life begins when you do right by YOU! I have your WORD, IT JUST HAD TO BE HEARD!

CPSIA information can be obtained
at www.ICGtesting.com
Printed in the USA
BVHW091124040922
646183BV00001B/1